Ancient Modocs of Califor[n]

D1603848

Carrol B. Howe

"I knew they had been here but I had to find the proof," Author Carrol Howe said of his search for clues of the ancient native Americans in California and Oregon. How the evidence was finally assembled after a 45-year search is told here in fascinating detail.

If these ancient Asiatic ancestors had been able to return to Nightfire Island and join their Modoc descendants, they would not have felt greatly handicapped in making a living. The Modoc people adapted to their surroundings rather than trying to change them—and a remarkable adaptation it was. Surviving in periods of drought and cold, they perpetuated a culture pattern that has provided an almost continuous scenario from the period of occupation of North America to the era of European contact.

True, the invention of the bow and arrow had revolutionized hunting, yet the techniques for making projectiles had changed but little. The elephant, then the bison and wolf, had disappeared, but other animals replaced them. Skins, reeds and grasses were still used for clothing. The methods of cooking were only slightly improved. The development of their extensive vocabulary is an indication of long years of occupation and communication. The survival skills must have been successfully passed along with little change.

It is remarkable that the setting for the entire story took place in the same region. These fierce people were able to defend and hold their territory against the pressure of the aggressive Paiutes, the Shastas and their Pit River neighbors. Whatever else may be discovered, it seems doubtful that any place will be found that was continuously occupied longer than the Modoc homeland.

The author's background in biological science has enabled him to describe the food resources of the Indians, including the waterfowl, plants, mammals and fish. He tells by pictures and words how they made the tools to gather, capture and prepare their food. He has traced some of the beliefs of the early Indians by studying the legends and language sources of the people. Professionals in archaeology, geology, physics, physical anthropology, and others have all contributed in drawing the composite picture of those remarkable Modocs of California and Oregon.

Ancient Modocs
of
California and Oregon

FOREWORD

This is an account of a land and a people. The land was high and cold. Its mountains had buckled and shifted. Some had erupted in volcanic explosions, others issuing flows of lava, pumice and obsidian. Its marshes and streams provided a habitat for waterfowl, plants and fish. The plains and forests were inhabited by mammals, some of which are now extinct.

The account of the people on this land concerns the way they survived for twelve to fifteen thousand years on the resources around them. Their adaptations by way of houses, weapons and inventions, along with the legends growing out of their struggle, go together to form a remarkable story.

This account also concerns the discoveries of a scientific group, their work put together for the purpose of finding out about the land and people. Each specialty has made its own contribution to new knowledge. The combination of the scientific reports aids in reconstructing a scene both original and ancient.

The author is greatly indebted to Dr. LeRoy Johnson, formerly of the University of Oregon; to Dr. Garth Sampson of Southern Methodist University, and to the team of scientists they assembled for the Nightfire Island study. They have generously shared their discoveries and interpretations.

In addition to thanking those mentioned in the text, I wish to thank the following who have made a contribution to my work: The Favell Museum; Dr. Bill Holm, University of Washington; Jim O'Donahue, naturalist; Van Landrum, engineer; Sharon Allen and Nora Gonzales De Rock, artists; Robert Rock, Juana and Terry Schafer, Audrey McPherson, Loraine Quillen, Sharon Poole, and especially my wife, Marjorie, for help in putting the information together. Without the consent and cooperation of the McKay family, there would have been no 4-SK-4 study and no book.

CONTENTS

INTRODUCTION

by *Patricia James Easterla*

In the midst of the Modoc War of 1873, a tiny wisp of life flickered into existence in a cave in Captain Jack's Stronghold, a natural lava fortress used by the Modocs in their determined battle against United States Government troops. Born to the Modoc warrior Shacknasty Jim and his wife Anna, this infant, my grandfather, survived that snowy, bloody winter and the arduous exile to Oklahoma Territory, the fate of the Modocs remaining at the end of the war.

The Modoc War, fought in what is today the Lava Beds National Monument, California, is a tale of tragic futility. The Modoc War also stands as a classic example of the fate of many American Indian groups. Eventually defeated, the Modocs went into exile as a totally dispirited and beaten people. Within a matter of a few decades, the Modocs, who had existed as a known group of people for thousands of years prior to the war, ceased to exist as a cultural unit.

Shacknasty Jim was the first of the exiled Modocs to express a desire for a Christian burial, rather than cremation upon his death in 1881. A converted Quaker, as were most of those transplanted Modocs, he left his possessions to his family rather than having them destroyed with him. He also left to his descendants the anglicized family name of James. But of his Modoc culture, little filtered down.

His son Clark was to grow to manhood in Oklahoma and like most of the Oklahoma Modocs was to know little of his ancestral roots. The mighty lava fortress, as well as the western homeland itself, was to be slowly lost to memory, replaced by the sprawling prairie and hardwood forests of the new land. The basket hats of the women were the last cultural remnant to die, the mists of time starting to cover remembrances of Tule Lake and its precious gift of tules.

One hundred and five years after the last shot of the Modoc War, I came to the Lava Beds National Monument to serve as a seasonal ranger-historian for the National Park Service. The Modoc blood of Shacknasty Jim and Anna had in three short generations mixed with blood stemming from Germany and Ireland, and the rigorous life of the early Modocs was by no means a way of life to me, only a history.

Yet the spirit of Modoc pride was there, transmitted by my father Clyde and by his German wife Luella, who preserved much of our family history. I have climbed down into every cave in the Stronghold, wondering if I have wandered into the one where my grandfather was born. I'll never know. But somehow I feel I have been at that spot.

My primary function as a ranger at the Lava Beds is to interpret for visitors—who come from all sections of the United States and abroad—the history of this area, opening people's minds and hopefully their hearts to the vast panorama of human social evolution. The silent, sagebrush-dotted Stronghold holds history locked in stone. To give substance and meaning to the Modocs who fought there is my job.

Carrol Howe, in *Ancient Modocs of California and Oregon*, has opened the earth itself to reveal the prehistory Modocs. It is fortunate that Howe appeared at the time and place in history that he did, combining his knowledge of the potential archaeological treasures that Nightfire Island might hold with his concern to preserve the site. The earth-bound secrets of the ancient Modocs could so easily have been erased.

The heart and the soul of the Modoc cannot be adequately interpreted without understanding the roots of their spirituality. The fierceness often found in Modoc theology and their never-ending endeavors to be at peace with their surroundings are foreign until the layers of Nightfire Island are peeled away, revealing the framework of their total way of life. Their harsh environment created not only a theological base, but a whole ethical and economic system that is difficult to comprehend when viewed without an understanding of the Modoc's age-old interaction with that environment.

Woven into sad discoveries, such as skeletons revealing the prevalence of *spina bifida* (the inability of the spinal vertebrae to close), are golden threads in the form of artifacts reflecting skill and artistry. Through this book, the primal Modoc begins to breathe and hunt and eat and worship — and create.

Too often the Modocs have been stigmatized as warring savages, with little thought or interpretation given to other facets of their culture. More than anything else, *Ancient Modocs of California and Oregon* has presented the Modocs as a solid, enduring people of great antiquity. Their tenacious staying power over thousands of years refutes their stereotype. They molded their culture to their environment, not the environment to themselves, and in this manner survived. They were fighters, but primarily they battled the environment, and when it was necessary to ally themselves with that environment, they could do that, too.

Often at dusk as I gaze across the Lava Beds, I conjure images of the shadowy, ancient Indians who lived in the lake lands adjoining the Lava Beds. What were they like?

I am comforted that, while much of Modoc knowledge and history was dying at the turn of the century, a small, as yet undiscovered island was patiently waiting to open its layers of centuries-old soil and tell its tale through the pen of Carrol Howe.

1. DISCOVERY OF NIGHTFIRE ISLAND

The Eruption

It must have happened in the spring, probably during the month of March or April. Spring in the Klamath country brings strong winds out of the southwest. Sweeping across the snowy heights of Mount Shasta, the air currents seem to increase in their frigid velocity as they howl toward the northeast.

The belief that spring was the time of the great eruption is based upon the fact that the fine pumice—now called Mount Mazama ash—was carried in a general northeasterly direction. It was blown from the mountain with such velocity that the ash layer has been found in seven western states and in three Canadian provinces. Each year new discoveries extend the known area blanketed by the eruption. The map, Fig. 1, is taken from information obtained in 1975.

Though a series of eruptions likely occurred, scientists have determined that the most violent explosion took place about 7,000 years ago. The date for the culminating eruption was established by making tests of charcoal (carbon 14) found with the pumice.

The exact length of time the eruptive explosions continued has not been established, but the impact of the explosions on the geography and plant life of the region is still felt. Mount Mazama continued spewing ash and pumice until the center of the mountain became hollow, Fig. 2. This once-tall peak, estimated to have been 12,500 feet high, then collapsed, leaving the beautiful

1

and awesome crater now known as Crater Lake. Later volcanic activity pushed a second small mountain, called a cinder cone, from the 4,000-foot depth of the caldera. This is now known as Wizard Island. Waters have filled the crater to a depth of about 2,000 feet, creating a beautiful, deep-blue lake, Fig. 3.

The effect of the falling ash upon wildlife must have been severe. Trees, grasses and shrubs were burned or buried. Studies by University of Oregon scientists have shown that some animal species which had occupied the Oregon desert disappeared completely, if not from the destruction, then from the loss of their food supply.

We now know that families were living in the region and were able to see the incandescent cloud rise and move toward them. Those in the Fort Rock Cave, about seventy miles northeast of the crater, had their cavern home and possessions completely covered by the pumice from the volcano. Indians living in Marmes Cave and Wind Dust Cave on the Columbia River, in the State of Washington, had a deep enough layer of Mazama ash fall upon them for future scientists to use the ash deposit as an indicator of the age of their habitation.

The blowup of the mountain must have been a terrifying experience for those living in the entire northwest region. As the earth shook and the skies darkened, there were likely many prayers, supplications and dances by medicinemen trying to appease the spirits which had inflamed the heart of the mountain. Evidence indicates that few, if any, of the cave residents were actually buried in the pumice, although the great depth of deposit near and to the north of Crater Lake leaves no doubt that every living thing nearby was destroyed. Those who could, left their habitations and most of their material possessions behind.

People living on the south shore of Lower Klamath Lake and their neighbors, the Shastas, must have been awe-struck by the rumbling explosions and earthquakes. Frightening though it was, the falling pumice had little effect on the lands of those tribes. The same winds, which had carried the towering cloud to destroy the habitat of the animals in the Fort Rock Valley, blew most of

Fig. 1. Many parts of Western America had been occupied prior to the
Mazama ash fall.

Fig. 2. An artist's conception of the Mazama eruption.
(National Park Service)

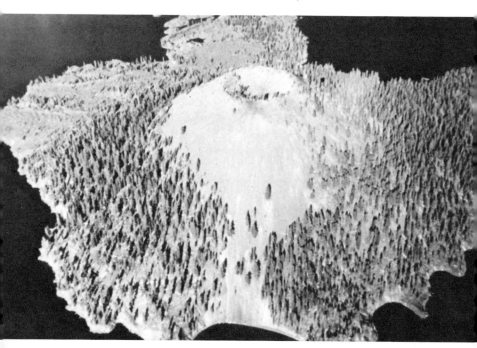

Fig. 3. Wizard Island, a volcano within a volcano.

the ash away from their villages. However, the earth-shaking volcano did have a decided effect on their homeland.

Lower Klamath Lake Goes Dry

Dr. LeRoy Johnson, archaeologist from the University of Oregon, who studied the region, believes that the eruption may have resulted in the slippage of the rock fault at Keno, where the Klamath River cuts its canyon through the Cascade Mountains. This ledge of rock controls the water levels of the Klamath River and the basin of Lower Klamath Lake. Only a slight lowering of the fault would cause the waters in the shallow basin to recede from the shores and leave the Modoc villages a considerable distance from their beloved marsh habitat. People who had gathered waterfowl eggs and fished from canoes found themselves land-locked. While the receding of the water could have also been caused by changes in climate, the result was the same—either the village had to be moved or a way of life altered.

The decision of the Indians was to move. Shortly after the pumice fall, the founders of what would come to be known as Nightfire Island moved onto the dry lakebed adjacent to the banks of today's Sheepy Creek. There the Mazama ash forms a thin layer on the lakebed muck to mark the occupation date when the first pioneers established the new village. Here canoes could be launched, fish could be caught and waterfowl captured.

One major disadvantage was that there were no rocks on the dry lakebed. Thousands of years of decaying vegetation, together with the gradual deposit of tiny white diatoms, had covered every portion of the lake bottom. The rocks had to be carried from nearby Sheepy Island. These Indian pioneers carried them—one by one, century after century—until they had, probably unintentionally, built an island about two and a half acres in extent. Over thousands of years, the patient occupants brought cooking stones for roasting pits. They also carried selected rocks for making mortars and pestles to the new village at the edge of the clear-flowing creek. To this was added the bones of the animals they had eaten, the charcoal from the fires, and the charred bones of their own dead, until the man-made island was built to a depth of over six feet above the lakebed. Contained within this accumulation was a record of adaptation to the climate of the Great Basin.

Water from the Cascades

The climate on the east side of the Cascade Mountains is decidedly different from that on the western side. Rainstorms blowing in from the Pacific Ocean lose most of the moisture as they pass over the mountain range. Average rainfall is six times greater on the west slope. Rainfall on the east in the Great Basin would hardly sustain any but a semi-desert type of plants and grasses. Fortunately for those who live on the east, the mountains catch the winter snows and the high-altitude temperatures preserve the snow pack long enough to allow a gradual melting rather than a quick runoff. On the shaded north slopes of Mount Shasta, a part of the snows are always preserved in the form of small glaciers. The slow-melting snows gradually sink into the porous soil to flow gradually through underground channels, then reappear in the form of springs. Melting snows feed the creeks flowing into the Sacramento River on the south and into the Klamath River on the west.

Great Basin Faulted Mountains

Lower Klamath Lake basin is at the meeting place where range-and-basin geological formations are joined by the Cascade Range. Interestingly, the bases of many of the faulted mountains here have been penetrated by the up-flowing, liquid-hot lava from beneath. As a result, waters penetrating the bases of these block-type mountains are heated and issue from the earth as warm spring or hot springs. One such fault on the north shore of the Lower Lake Basin in Oregon was drilled as a potential geothermal site.

Sheepy Creek rises near the edge of such a block fault, then flows crystal clear toward the north past another block fault called Sheepy Island. On the way it is joined by other springs, each adding to the volume until the water flow compares to that of a small river. The spring nearest to Nightfire Island has warm water and is presently used for irrigation. Some geothermal springs in the region of Klamath Falls had a temperature that was high enough to be used by the Indians for cooking. The Nightfire spring was not that hot but it may have provided a warm place to add to the comfort of the Indians during the cold winter season.

During the more than 7,000 years that have passed since the village was founded, many changes took place. The layered earth structure of the island shows that there were long time periods when the island was abandoned, perhaps for hundreds of years or for a thousand. At times the lake rose and ducks left their droppings to form a distinct yellow layer in the earth. The climate changed; perhaps the rock fault at Keno changed. Sandy layers mixed with rock show how waves washed at the island. During other periods, the waters would recede and again the Indians would return to leave a deposit, black with charcoal from the cooking and cremation fires.

Numerous waterfowl bones indicate that the first occupants hunted them. In other periods, they indicate that the lakebed may have become a grassy plain crossed by the watercourses of the few creeks that drained toward the Klamath River.

Like the pages of an ancient book, each layer of soil contained its own history. Each stratum held the answers to many of the questions about those who had lived and died there. To get the answers, the efforts of many different scientific skills and specialties were required. The story proved to be truly revealing but, for the author, many agonizing moments, months, and years of time, plus hours of hard labor, would be required before the answers would be found. Even now, some questions are unanswered.

Since first coming to the Klamath country in 1930, I had been interested in the Indian people, their educational progress and their heritage. A student, Charles Cowan, who was a member of the Klamath Tribe, brought to school some of the arrowheads, knives and flaked objects which he had found while herding sheep in the Modoc area near Tule Lake. This further increased an already active curiosity about the early history of the Indians.

With others, I encouraged the establishment of a county museum to preserve and display the natural features of the region. While I served as a museum commission member, limited archaeological studies were carried on with some of the museum curators.

In 1958, a friend told me about an Indian campsite that had been discovered near the dry bed of Lower Klamath Lake. This created no great excitement, as the old lakeshores were virtually a continuous archaeological zone. Two years later, a visit with the owner of the property was arranged and permission was asked to examine the site. The owner, Mr. John McKay, courteously told me that I could visit the property but that no digging would be permitted as there were cremated bones in the soil. He felt that, although the earth was being used for the construction of irrigation dams and dikes, there should be no disturbance of the earth except where it was necessary to carry out this work. (It should be mentioned here that most of the islands on Lower Klamath had previously been leveled for agricultural purposes or for building sites.) I was given directions on how to find the place where an irrigation dam was built. Winding through the ranch properties, I left Sheepy Island, and it was with some disappointment that I drove onto the lakebed, on arrival at the creek. My assumption had been that any Indian occupation of significance would be on the shore of Sheepy Island.

The Village

When I reached the dam, I was amazed. The earth-movers had uncovered a low mound, black with charcoal and interspersed with cooking rocks and broken stone tools. Here and there was a scattered arrowhead or seashell bead. The mound, directly adjacent to the creek, had been inaccessible by land until the railroad fill at Ady caused the lake to go dry. I tried to visualize the setting as it would have been a few centuries ago: a village, well hidden by tules and cattails, accessible to raiding parties only by canoe, with ample fresh water from Sheepy Creek, plus an unobstructed channel into the lake. The only thing lacking would be firewood. (At this time, it was thought that the island was built upon a ledge of native rock.) The scene was intriguing. In 1888, Albert Gatschet described his reactions to the Klamath country in his "Ethnographic Sketch of the People." He wrote:

"The pure azure sky and the perpetual silence of nature reigning in these uplands add impressions of grandeur which it is impossible to describe. . .Noiselessly the brooks and streams pursue their way through the purifying volcanic sands; the murmur of the waves and the play of the water-birds, interrupted at times by the cry of a solitary bird, are the only noises to break the silence. Beyond the few settlements of the Indian and away from the post-road, scarcely any trace of the hand of man reminds us of the existence of human beings. There nature alone speaks to us, and those who are able to read history in the formations in the steeper ledges of this solitary corner of the globe will find ample satisfaction in their study."

Gatschet spent two years with the Klamaths, Modocs and Yahooskin Snakes. His mission was to study the language of the resident Indians for the U.S. Bureau of Ethnology. This he did very well. He also made many observations about the way of life and physical settings of the Indian culture that have been of lasting value.

Where the Sun and the Moon Live

Gatschet's informants revealed that the crescent-shaped ridge (now called Sheepy Island) on the map was called Shapasheni by the Modocs, meaning "where the sun and moon live." The Indian camp located there at the beginning of the historic period was also called by that name. Many Indian names are unpronounceable except by Indians. Old-timers had undoubtedly tried and failed, and then decided to pronounce Shapasheni as sheepy. And so it is—the name of the creek and island on all maps is Sheepy.

In Fig. 4 the end of crescent-shaped Sheepy Island shows at the upper right. The creek flows into Sheepy Lake at the upper left. Nightfire Island shows as a faint white area on the bank of the creek. To the south lies the beautiful snowy spine of Mt. Shasta, first named by the Hudson's Bay trapper, Peter Skene Ogden. To

SHEEPY]

↑
NIGHTFIRE IS.

↑
SHEEPY CREE

Fig. 4. Where the sun and moon live. The Lower Klamath Lake Basin lies north of Nightfire Island.

Fig. 5. Johnson does careful mapping and planning prior to excavation.

Fig. 6. Highwater marks, as well as levels and altitude, were determined by Van Landrum, engineer.

the north is the town of Midland where the former Modoc village Stuikisheni (at the canoe bay) was located. North and east were the former island camps where the U.S. Fish and Wildlife buildings were constructed.

Farther east looms the white face of the chalkbank, where early-day steamboats landed with lumber for the citizens in the city of Merrill, Oregon. From all these places, as well as from the nearby Modoc village at Otey Island, the fires of Shapasheni would light the skies as they burned to cook the meals, to warm the closely huddled families on cold nights, and at times to cremate the bodies of the dead. Sheepy seemed a poor name for all this, so I decided to call it Nightfire Island in remembrance of those scenes which had taken place so frequently in past centuries.

My vists to Nightfire were infrequent during the first two years after the initial trip. On each occasion that I returned, I was both enthralled and agonized: enthralled with the location and environment of the village and the many ways it helped to sustain human life; and agonized by curiosity over the clues which were revealed when the earth was pulled away to repair the dams and dikes. The soil, almost black in color, contained a rich content of animal bones, the bones of birds, and an occasional artifact of obsidian or stone.

Even more exciting, where the bands of soil were left in a vertical condition, the definite bands of changing color and texture indicated lines of stratification. It is unusual to find a stratified condition in the dry, windy climate of the Great Basin country except in caves. The clear waters of the creek, too, revealed tantalizing evidence of the former residents: on the creek bottom I found a broken pipe, shell beads, a pestle, even a bone gamecall, more than enough to fan the flames of my imagination.

As I made occasional visits to the Sheepy Island ranch, my friendly relationship with the McKay family had continued. Finally, driven by curiosity, I mustered the courage to ask permission to screen the dirt to be removed, before it was placed in the dikes for repairs. I suppose John McKay thought I was crazy, but finally, perhaps in pity, he allowed me to further my study of the island. He said that no human bones should be removed from the site and that any soil studied should be replaced. I was delighted; my feet didn't touch the ground for several days.

As I examined the soils of the mound, it was as expected, stratified with an unusual occurrence of artifacts in some strata, almost none in others. Where the earth had been scraped away, there appeared to be a native residual bedrock with broken fragments mixed with yellowish sand. As the rocky layer was extremely hard to penetrate, my efforts were concentrated on the softer, easier portions of the midden.

On one occasion, I was accompanied to the island by my son, George. At that time, he was a student at the University of Oregon and was employed part-time in paleontology research by Dr. Arnold Shotwell. I explained to him that the rocky layer of the island was from an outcrop rising from the bottom, simply fragments of native basalt. He insisted in trying to find out why the rock formation occurred there. Laboriously, and over the objections of a complaining father, we removed a small square and found the neck bone of a large mammal. We also discovered that the rocks were not bedrock but had been carried there. Beneath them was a layer of yellow sand and charcoal, then the white clay-like soil which made up the bottom of the old lakebed—our first discovery that the island had been built by human hands upon the bottom of a lake!

A Site of Major Importance

It was apparent that this Indian village was unusual, perhaps unique. My memory of finding the artifacts in association with fossil camelbones on the dry lakebed of Lower Klamath Lake came back to stimulate my imagination. It was now also apparent that Nightfire Island was too important a site for me to investigate. Amateur archaeologists can help further scientific knowledge by locating and describing sites. They can also destroy by their lack of the skills and techniques which are necessary to make scientific investigation. It was obvious that I should try to get permission for professional research people to work on the site. After the potential value of the site was explained, the McKay family agreed to allow me to invite archaeologists from the University of Oregon to investigate. They also said that they would not remove any more of the island for construction purposes until after the research team had done the excavation.

The science of archaeology has undergone marked changes since the days when a lone professor would go into the wilderness with a group of students to excavate, collect, study, then return to the university in the fall. Present-day archaeological methods require a team of scientific professionals to be assembled from different departments of a university. They may even include specialists from several institutions. Such recruitment depends upon the needs for the special field of study. Financing such an effort usually calls for more money that the meager operating budgets allocated to college departments of anthropology or university museums.

This proved to be the case when the writer invited David Cole, head of the archaeology department at the University of Oregon, to investigate and study Nightfire Island. Since personal observations had convinced me that the stratified site could be of real importance, it was felt that an effort should be made to help Mr. Cole finance at least an investigation of the strata in the mound. As a member of the Klamath County Museum Commission, I requested a budget grant from the county commissioners to fund a modest project. The sympathetic answer was, of course, that the requirements of county government services left little choice in the allocation of funds.

Finance for a Research Study

A burning thirst to find out the truth about what was contained within and under the rocky sands of Nightfire led me to make an effort to get a special research grant from the state legislature for the Oregon Museum of Natural History. My fellow-legislators gave me a sympathetic hearing and some enthusiastic praise, but no funds for the state museum. A suggestion from Mary Elizabeth

Hansell, wife of the chairman of the Ways and Means Committee, led to the discovery of a proposed law previously introduced in the legislature. This bill provided a grant of highway fund money (gas tax) for county museums. A little amending was required since the bill as written applied only to the county represented by the original sponsors. As amended, a grant would be given to those counties where a museum was maintained and met certain other standards. The path of progress was rough. It is not easy to get state money, much less easy to take it away from a powerful existing agency.

With the help of the original sponsors, the museum aid bill finally passed by one vote. It was written to provide $5,000 a year on a matching basis. Different portions of that amount (never the full amount) have filtered down to those counties maintaining approved public museums. Flushed with success from the legislative effort, another approach was made to the county commissioners. This time, $1,300 of the money allocated by the state was budgeted for research at Nightfire.

David Cole visited the mound with the author and called for a preliminary study to determine if the site (now given the unglamorous title 4-SK-4) had the potential for a full-fledged scientific investigation and research project. University of Oregon archaeologists added to the joy of the writer by adopting the name Nightfire Island. This name now appears in the scientific journals and papers reporting the findings made there. Fig. 5 shows Dr. LeRoy Johnson with the author preparing maps of the island prior to beginning the excavation.

The words of Dr. Johnson will best describe the findings of this first limited investigation: "A week of test investigation in 1966 revealed a series of geologic and cultural strata rich in artifacts, faunal remains, charcoal, and other occupational detritus. The bottom stratum is lacustrine, diatom-rich silt which represents the original lake floor upon which the first occupation occurred. This member is overlain by a series of local lenses of silt, stream-sand, and loam variously endurated (forming duripan) or unaltered. Cultural debris reaches a maximum of 3 m. The site prom-

ised to help unravel Klamath Basin prehistory because of its
discrete occupational components and its apparently long history,
which appeared to extend back beyond the peak of the Hypsithermal [over 7,000 years]."

From this preliminary study, it was determined that there was
much to be learned at 4-SK-4. An application was made by J. Arnold Shotwell, director of the Museum of Natural History, to the
National Science Foundation for a grant to make the study. The
grant became G.S. 1413 and the probe into the past history
began. Dr. Johnson, who was then curator of ethnology at the
museum, was selected to direct the research project. Preparations
were made for the excavation and field study in the year 1966.
Eight University of Oregon students were hired to carry out the
field work. All students were selected because anthropology was
their major field of interest. The owners of the property, the
McKay family, gave the field team the greatest cooperation, even
keeping all cattle out of the pasture during the time the excavations were in progress.

Johnson Directs the Work

During the field work, Johnson made investigative trips, sometimes accompanied by the author, into the region surrounding the
site. His object was to see if there were relationships in the geology, fauna, or archaeological evidence with the people who built
the island.

Engineering data on 4-SK-4 was provided by a registered engineer, Van Landrum, Fig. 6, who donated his work to the project.
Data included the approximate highwater mark of Lower
Klamath Lake, the altitude and lowest depth of occupation. The
site was then staked, after being laid out in squares, so that any
specimens found could be related to the horizontal location on the
island. In the words of Dr. Johnson: "Site 4-SK-4 was excavated
according to the interval sampling technique. The low occupation mound was penetrated by twenty-three 2-by-2m. excavation
pits which extended to a maximum depth of 3.0 m. below the site

Fig. 7. Distinctive stratification is pointed out by Dr. Johnson.

Fig. 8. Bags were labeled so the island could be reconstructed in the laboratory.

Fig. 9. Dr. Garth Sampson of Southern Methodist University rechecks the site.

surface. The excavation yield was almost twice as large as antici-
pated, consisting of projectile points, flake knives and scrapers,
all of obsidian; pecked basalt mortars and pestles, as well as a
number of basalt manos and grinding slabs; bone and antler
wedges, beads, etc.; shell beads, and other shell ornaments; rich
faunal remains; 30 burials; and two early circular house structures. Also collected were soil, pollen, faunal, obsidian, and charcoal samples." Fig. 7 shows Dr. Johnson examining the stratification of the man-made island.

The depth or vertical levels of the site were divided into seventeen levels so that the exact position and relationship of the
materials could be located for permanent record and future
reference.

Despite mosquitoes, sun and horseflies, the university team
cheerfully entered into the slow, painstaking process of collecting
and coding any piece of bone, rock or artifact that could be of
value in telling the story of the Nightfire people. Johnson gave
careful supervision to the various pairs who worked the different
pits in the grid system. Materials removed were immediately
placed in coded brown paper bags, Fig. 8, so that the contents of
the soil could be viewed in the same relationship in which they
were found. Friendly competition helped the students forget the
sore muscles and sunburned backs. At the end of the digging
season, materials which had been collected and carefully labeled
were returned to the university. There in the laboratory the
reconstruction of past ages began.

The assembling of the parts of the story has been a long and difficult process. Changes in personnel at the university took place.
Dr. Johnson resigned and turned the project over to Dr. Garth
Sampson. Dr. Sampson moved to Southern Methodist University
in Dallas, Texas, but continued the research. He returned to con-
fer with the author, to make drawings of the Nightfire collection
and further examine the soils of the island. Fig. 9 shows him at
the island with archaeologist Linda Verrett of Southern Methodist University.

Without the scientific studies and information from Dr. Johnson and Dr. Sampson, the story of the Nightfire people contained in this book could not have been told. The charts, graphs and research reports will prove an important contribution to our knowledge of the American Indian.

2. THE CRADLE

The First Americans

America has been discovered a number of times. The most famous discovery, of course, was made by Columbus. Certainly it was also discovered by the Norsemen. Some believe that Japanese pottery makers landed on the west coast of South America even before the Norsemen. There is strong evidence that Irish monks led by St. Brenden reached the west shores of the Atlantic in a rawhide boat. Artifacts and structures found in Mexico suggest both Egyptian and Middle Eastern influence. The black stone object in Fig. 10 has a beetle-shaped back and human face similar to Egyptian scarabs.

No one is sure of the exact time of the first discovery of America. Estimates of scientists range from 15,000 to 35,000 years ago. Some believe that an occupation took place even earlier. Improved methods of establishing the age of artifacts have tended to push back the time of discovery. While there is disagreement about the time the first migrants arrived, there are many facts surrounding these events that are generally accepted.

Most scientists agree that it took place at a time when the earth was much colder, so cold that much of the ocean's water was held in the form of ice. This resulted in the water levels being lower than today—so low, in fact, that a land bridge connected Asia and North America where Siberia and Alaska are now separated by Bering Strait. If the land bridge did not provide a pathway,

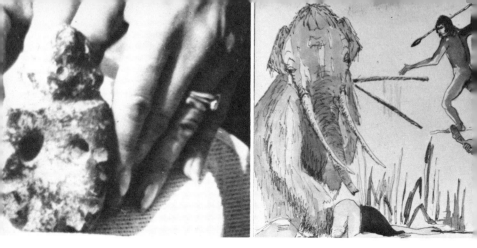

Fig. 10. The beetle-back on this statuette resembles those
on Egyptian scarabs.

Fig. 11. Mastodon hunters ambushed game with Clovis points.

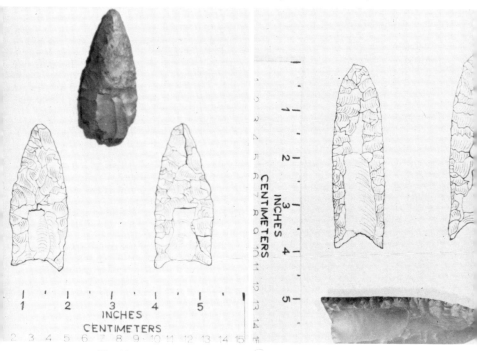

Fig. 12. Mammoth Spring Clovis found in the Lost River Circle.

Fig. 13. Merganser Clovis from Lost River Slough.

certainly the simplest watercraft could have made the short voyage.

A second point of agreement about the first human beings to enter America is that they were Asians called Mongoloids. They formed the racial stock of what we now call American Indians. Over thousands of years, there developed diverse languages, tribes and living habits but the basic Asian characteristics remain.

The Hunters

Archaeologists also agree on other features of America's first discovery. The Asian pioneers were hunters of large animals. There was no mass migration, no planned landing, no effort to establish colonies. They came in small groups, probably families, skirting along the edges of the receding glaciers, more driven by hunger than a sense of adventure or an effort to populate the Americas with their kind.

Many of the animals that they chased are now extinct. Among those found along with the artifacts of man were camels, elephants (both mastodon and mammoth), the giant ground sloth, the giant *Bison antiquus* and a form of the peccary. Evidence found in Fells Cave in South America indicates that if these first Americans had not been so hungry and eaten the horses, they might have domesticated the animal thousands of years before the Spanish explorers brought the riding horse to the Indians. The wandering hunters did, however, have one domestic animal—the dog, which was brought from Asia. The range of the hunter's activities extended clear to the tip of South America. New discoveries each year increase the number of sites they are known to have occupied.

Scientists at the National Museum of Anthropology in Mexico believe that the success of the hunters was so great that they helped to bring about the extinction of some large animal species in North America, including the *Bison antiquus*, horse, camel, mastodon, mammoth and ground sloth.

Passing from Alaska, through Alberta, Canada, the first ancient people left sufficient artifacts at the kill-sites that they could be identified and classified according to age. H.M. Wormington, of Denver, has become a recognized authority on ancient artifacts after a lifetime of study of the Great Basin area. Other studies of the caves of Oregon, Nevada and New Mexico have added to the fund of information about these people.

Certain types of artifacts have been associated with certain groups of animal hunters. The Clovis-type point, first found in association with elephant bones near Clovis, New Mexico, has become a trademark of elephant hunters. The Folsom point has been determined to be a later invention and has become associated with the extinct *Bison antiquus*. The most recent discovery in the Northwest, made near Sequim, Washington, was a mastodon skeleton. David Daugherty of Washington State University said that one of the elephant bones still contained part of a bone projectile or spear.

The period of time when one of the wandering bands of hunters entered the Great Basin of Western America has become known as the Post-Glacial. The flat basins now occupied by lakes and salt flats were much deeper. The region received much more rainfall and supported vegetation used by the herds of large mammals. As the Great Basin became drier, both herds and hunters had to seek a wider range.

The First Californians?

It is only natural that these hunters should have moved toward the western edge of the basin where waters flowing eastward from the Cascade Range made a suitable habitat. The bones of mastodon and *Bison antiquus* have been known to exist in Northern California and Oregon for a long time. In 1934, the author found fossil bones identified as camel, in association with projectile points, but did not dream that human beings could co-exist with the extinct camel. Both the bones and associated artifacts were given to the University of Oregon.

The recent discovery by university scientists of a llama-like camel, together with projectile points at Fossil Lake, led to an inquiry. A call to Dr. L.S. Cressman, former head of the anthropology department and an authority on ancient man, led to the answer that he believed most certainly that the camel and human beings lived at the same time on the Lower Klamath Lake Basin. Were these hunters who left their fossil-bone foreshafts and crudely chipped objects at the camel kill-site the first Californians?

Elephant Hunters in Oregon and California

It is only recently that sufficient proof of ancient man has been found to show that a group of the first Californians probably lived and thrived in the northeastern part of that state. A part of this proof is the clovis-type point shown in Fig. 11. This specimen was examined by Wormington who said, "It certainly has all the attributes of the true clovis point." Dr. Garth Sampson of Southern Methodist University described it as "a textbook example of a clovis." The set of artifacts and way of life associated with the early elephant hunters has become known as the Llano culture, after the plains over which they roamed. The Llano people did not subsist entirely on elephants. They are known to have used some plantfoods and other animals. The trademark of the clovis hunter is the flake removed from each side of the chipped projectile point, called a fluted point. The yellow jasper point pictured has the typical "ears" broken off the back. Wormington suggested that possibly it had been reworked for use as a scraper.

The place where this and other evidence of the Llano culture has been discovered is at Clear Lake and its tributary, Lost River. There are many named Clear Lakes but one of the most unclear is the large one in northern Modoc County, California. It was once called Ben Wright's Lake after the early Indian fighter from Yreka. Why the name was changed is not known but perhaps because of Wright's unsavory reputation with the Modoc, Shasta and Rogue River Indians. In any case, the name should be changed again. First, the lake is not and never has been clear; and second, because it is almost always confused with the much better known Clear Lake in Lake County, California.

Clear Lake in Modoc County was once skirted by the Applegate Trail leading to Oregon and California. Later, the Carr ranch—established about the time of the Modoc War—was located at its edge. In its natural condition, the vast basin was principally marshland. Fed by springs, it provided a most favorable habitat for both animals and birds. It also must have provided an ideal bog for the entrapment or ambush of the large beasts driven to their doom by the barking dogs and the spears of the native Americans, Fig. 12.

About the year 1910, the United States Bureau of Reclamation constructed its dam on Lost River at the outlet of Clear Lake. Its purpose was to hold back the waters from the rich farm lands of the Tule Lake Basin. The construction of the dam greatly increased the size and depth of the former marsh. The marshes and grass plants were killed. As the water fluctuated in depth, the forces of erosion—wind, waves and ice, especially ice—cut into the exposed shores revealing the artifacts and weapons accumulated there over thousands of years. The grinding, wind-blown icepacks not only exposed these ancient tools, but also mixed many of them together, making the identification and dating by stratification virtually impossible.

One rose does not make a rose garden; one clovis point, although positively identified by authorities, does not prove the presence of the Llano culture. Western Indians are known to have traded over a wide range. It was entirely possible that the yellow clovis point in my possession could have been traded from New Mexico. Further evidence was needed to establish the Clear Lake-Lost River Circle as a habitat for North America's most ancient people. This evidence has been provided by the recent discovery of a more perfect clovis-type point by Dr. Rodney Wright, county agricultural agent of Burns, Oregon, Fig. 13.

This clovis-type point was found on the bank of a large canal built to divert the waters of Lost River from its channel into the Klamath River. The canal followed the natural grade of the old Lost River Slough, which formed a connection for the two rivers in times of high water. Since it was discovered near the old townsite of Merganser, it is called the Merganser Point. It is four inches long and made of a dense black material more like basalt than most obsidian. The ancient point was brought to the surface from a deeper layer and laid on the bank by the dredging operation. This find proved that the first clovis point was no accident and that the Llano people had lived in the region of the Lost River Circle.

The bones of the mastodon have been found in the vicinity of the Lost River Slough; also the fossilized horn core of *Bison antiquus*. So far, no positive association has been found between these fossils and the tools of man. The fossil tracks of the ground sloth have been found near Drew's Valley in Lake County, Oregon, about forty-two miles from Clear Lake, but there is no evidence that the animal was pursued or eaten by men.

Further signs of the ancient culture at Clear Lake are illustrated by the bone cylinders shown in Fig. 14. The bluish bones were found near Mammoth Springs where the clovis point was discovered. Such tools have been found in Llano sites and at Marmes Cave in Washington. The bones pictured are different from the foreshafts discovered near the camel bones at Lower Klamath Lake, as the latter were beveled.

Before the Bow and Arrow

Further evidence that the Lost River Circle was the setting for early man is to be found in the enormous numbers of small football-shaped stones, shown in top of Fig. 15. These have been found around Clear Lake and along the shores of Lost River. They have previously been described as gaming stones, dog rocks and sling stones. Some are crudely made; others are well finished. Dr. H.H. Stuart of Eureka, California, was the first to suggest that they were bolas stones. He presented the author with four similar weights made of clay found on the coast of California, bottom Fig. 15. Stuart theorized that Indians used them to catch birds. This explanation certainly went along well with conditions surrounding the Clear Lake stones: for example, their location near

Fig. 14. Bone cylinders have been found in association with ancient points.

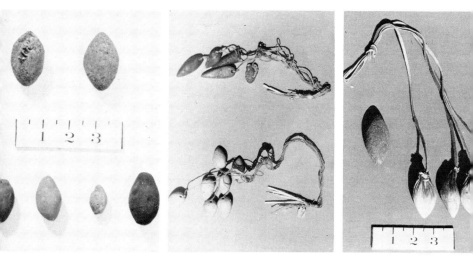

Fig. 15. (left). Football-shaped bolas stones shown with clay balls from California coast. Fig. 16. (center). Northwest Coast bolas sets from the Burke Museum, University of Washington. Fig. 17. (right). Method of mounting bolas stones in rawhide bags.

Fig. 18. Rare notched-bolas stone in Favell Museum.

water, sometimes in groups, streamlined for throwing, and far too numerous for use as gambling stones.

The problem of proof was finding a method by which the stones were attached to the string. A visit to the Burke Museum at the University of Washington showed that while most Northwest Indian bolas weights were shaped in a similar manner to those of the Klamath region, all northwest weights were bored on one end for attachment to the string, Fig. 16. These sets contained from four to seven weights. The sinew or gut cordage was controlled in flight by a group of feathers or a small stone which served in the same way the tail holds a kite in proper position. This also could well have served to help recover the missile when it fell into the water.

Mr. Del Davis of Lakeview, Oregon, has watched the Northwest Indians capture geese in flight by using the bolas. He said that the hunters carried the sets draped over the left shoulder and by throwing with the right arm could put two bolas sets into the air before the birds escaped.

In an attempt to find a method of attachment for the Clear Lake stones, the author constructed an animal skin capsule of rawhide and strung it with buckskin, Fig. 17. Strangely enough, much later information was found which verified the accidental discovery. In his *Archaeology of South America*, T. Athol Joyce states: "The bolas stones, of which numbers have been found, are well made and beautifully symmetrical. The smaller stones are of more than one pattern—both bi-conical and spherical examples have been found but their method of attachment was different since they were enclosed in a *small hide bag* to which the cord was fastened."

It would seem that enclosing the missiles in a skin bag was easier than drilling a hole through the stone, although one specimen in the Favell Museum in Klamath Falls, Oregon, has been notched on both ends to hold the cordage in place. This is a most unusual case, Fig. 18.

These football-shaped objects are different from the stones found in the early levels of culture on the Columbia River. The

Fig. 19. Using the bolas on waterfowl.

Fig. 20. Old blade from Lost River culture, Modoc County, California.

Fig. 21. Shouldered basalt point, basally ground.

latter were about the same weight but had grooves cut around them to hold the bolas string in place. The sketch, Fig. 19, shows the method of using the bolas described by Mr. Davis.

Antiquity of the Bolas

There is no doubt that the American Indians used the bolas for the thousands of years before the invention or introduction of the bow and arrow in both North and South America. Proof of this great antiquity was found when Junius Bird excavated Fells Cave in Argentina. Here he found bolas stones in association with the remains of the extinct sloth, the native American horse and small camels. Bird's study also disclosed that the horse was eaten by the Patagonians rather than ridden. He may have also found the original ancestors of the "bolo"—now used in a much larger form by the gauchos or Argentine cowboys.

The tremendous numbers of bolas stones exposed by the forces of erosion at Clear Lake must indicate that they were used over many years of occupation and also that the area supported vast numbers of waterfowl. Strangely enough, there is almost no evidence of a fishing culture at the lake itself, although the banks of Lost River show that fishing there was popular. Currently the islands in the lake provide a nesting place for white pelicans and terns and are off limits to visitors.

Roots of the Modoc

What finally happened to the Llano (Clovis) people? Did they simply wander off into extinction or disappear when the elephants and large animals became too few to support their way of life? The answer seems to be that they did not. The succession of old spear and dart points found there shows that more likely the atlatl-propelled dart replaced the hand spear and that other smaller animals such as antelope, bison, muledeer and bighorn sheep replaced the elephant and the *Bison antiquus*.

In the churned-up sands of the lake shores, various types of early projectile points have come to light, indicating that occupation of the region continued with some slight changes over a great

Fig. 22. Brown jasper point, basally ground.

Fig. 23. Lost River Circle points.

Fig. 24. Crude stone metate with multifaceted mano.

Fig. 25. Bathtub-shaped metate for specialized grinding.

Fig. 26. Quern stones, sometimes called foot pestles.

Fig. 27. These mortars were used with quern stones.

time span. The projectile point in Fig. 20 is believed by the author to have considerable age. Made of a chert-like material, it was nearly covered by a heavy mineral deposit. Despite various efforts to remove the deposit, some of it remains.

Another specimen, Fig. 21, made of a basalt-like material, has a Sandia-type shoulder and shows basal grinding. The brown jasper point in Fig. 22 has basal grinding and resembles some Windust Cave specimens in shape, but the workmanship is finer. Since the Windust-phase culture has been found at Christmas Lake in Lake County, Oregon, it seems odd that it has never appeared in the Lost River-Clear Lake area.

Neither specimen in Fig. 23 shows basal grinding but the point goes back into antiquity. The side notch spear is much larger than the side notch points more common to the region.

The Llano people did not subsist entirely upon animal foods nor did those who followed them in the time span. The crude, ridged metate in Fig. 24 shows that plant foods were gathered and ground on a milling stone. The multi-faced mano (hand-grinding stone) is a type common in the Clear Lake region but rare on other sites. In contrast to the crude specimens is the finely shaped platter in Fig. 25. Made of volcanic rock, it appears to have been designed to grind a particular type of plant food.

The numerous shapes, sizes and quality of the working tools in the Clear Lake watershed are an indication that a variety of plants was gathered. The actual tons of grinding stones, which the elements have eroded from the shores, indicate the many thousands of years that were required for their manufacture and deposit.

A grinding stone which appears in the Cradle Culture rather frequently, but is rare in other Indian campsites, is the stone in Fig. 26. This stone, for lack of a better name, was called a foot pestle by both amateur and professional students of archaeology. The exact method of usage is unknown, but recent discovery has provided valuable new information about the use of these stones, as well as confirming the antiquity of their users.

The Lost River, after leaving Clear Lake, makes a rapid descent through a steep canyon, then enters Langell Valley in Oregon. Winding down through the town of Bonanza, it has cut through a fault block-ridge at a place called Harpold Dam. The river banks show extensive Indian occupation all along the course, but both banks of the narrows at Harpold Dam were for centuries the favored fishing place during the spring mullet run. The river bottom here was shallow where the stream crossed the rock fault of the ridge. The dip net and spear could be used effectively by the wading fishermen. Even the higher ridges show archaeological artifacts, perhaps from a period of flood stage, perhaps during post-glacial times before the channel was cut so deep.

The Quern Discovery

Mr. William LaVerne, owner of the property below Harpold Dam, was using land-leveling heavy equipment to grade the site for farming. When he uncovered a stratum of alluvial soil, his blade grated on a rock. Lifting it out, he determined that it was an Indian mortar. Shortly afterward he struck another mortar and recovered it. It is not unusual to find these stones anywhere along the course of the river but the two he found here were most unusual, Fig. 27. The author was invited to inspect the stones and found they had obviously been used for two purposes—as a regular mortar and as a special mortar. A shallow basin had been ground on each side near the bottom of the mortars. The depressions were obviously not made by a pestle or maul—they were a perfect nesting place for the "foot pestles." We now know they were querns or grinding stones which were used in a circular motion like millstones. Early housewives of the Lost River Valley must have determined to make double-purpose kitchen implements suitable for grinding dried fish and duck meat in one season, small grass seed in another.

There have been other mortars which show signs of use as the base element of the quern, but none so clearly as to positively identify the purpose. It seems probable that many of the stones which were identified by the author in *Ancient Tribes of the Klamath Country* as "Lazy-Wife" mortars were also part of a quern.

Mystery of the Crescents

Additional evidence of the great age of the Modocs in their Clear Lake-Lost River habitat is to be found in the presence of the chipped-stone crescents. It has been discovered by Cressman and others that these stones were made and used more than 13,000 years ago by the people who inhabited Fort Rock Cave in South-eastern Oregon. Such stones are also present in other older Great Basin sites, as well as in the ancient San Dieguito culture in California. The use, or uses, of these chipped objects still remains a mystery. The writer once believed them to be a part of the magic kit used by the Indian conjurers for ceremonial purposes or in the healing arts.

Certain specimens in the California State Museum are said to have been worn by medicine men to represent the claws of the bear. Those crescents found in the ancient Great Basin regions do not seem to fit such a pattern. They are found most often on the wind-blown beds of the dry desert lakes. Strangely enough, they were most frequently made of agate, jasper or colored stone, while other chipped artifacts were normally made of obsidian. All but one of those in Fig. 28 have been ground in the center portion. This suggests attachment to cordage for fishing, or to a thong to be worn as an ornament.

Although the purpose of the crescents remains a mystery, their presence has become a valuable diagnostic measure of age in the Great Basin area of the West. By the time the Modocs moved to Nightfire Island, these stone objects had gone out of style. The small crescent in lower Fig. 28 is from Nightfire Island but it does not resemble the older Clear Lake pieces in either size, shape or material.

15,000 Years of Adaptation

It is unfortunate that a complete multi-discipline study of the Lost River Circle has never been made. The author arranged for

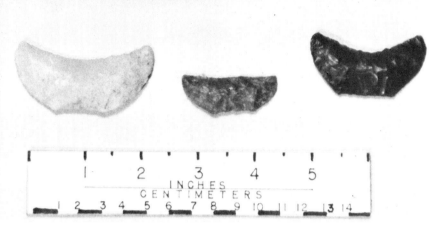

Fig. 28. Crescents from the Cradle Culture are different from the small one from Nightfire.

Fig. 29. An ancient site emerges as Clear Lake lowers.

Dr. LeRoy Johnson to do survey work there but water levels were never such that the study could be carried out. It is fortunate that the culture shows a positive overlap into the Nightfire Island culture described in the following chapters. The identical elements of the Nightfire culture serve to establish the continuous progression of the occupation. The missing elements provide a time-span cutoff to prove the changes that occurred prior to the occupation of Nightfire Island.

The few positive remnants of the Llano culture that have been saved from the forces of erosion give testimony that those intrepid elephant hunters, who roamed through the basins of Central America, may have very well founded the stock for one of America's oldest areas of permanent occupation.

If the Llano people lived and hunted and died in the Clear Lake watershed from 12,000 to 15,000 years ago, then what happened? Were they driven from the region by others? Were they exterminated by volcanoes or other natural forces? The answer seems to be that they, or certainly other ancient tribes, stayed in the Lost River Circle and adapted their tools and weapons to the available resources to establish the region as a "Cradle" from which future generations would develop.

In some dry year, when the barren, rocky earth emerges from the lowering lake, as in Fig. 29, we may find proof that this was the oldest continuously occupied Indian camp in Western America.

3. LIFE FROM THE SKY

Waterfowl Economy

Indian tribes often became closely identified with the principal type of food on which they lived. Indians in Oregon were called the Calapooias "camas burners"; one Paiute branch was called "woodchuck eaters." The Sioux became famous as "buffalo people," the Hohokam were "corn people," the Hupa, the "salmon people." Certainly a fitting name for the Nightfire Modocs would be the "waterfowl people."

Although the amount of local rainfall was meager, there was much open water and marsh habitat for waterfowl. The basins between the fault-block ridges held water in the marshes, and the Cascade Range provided a barrier that controlled outflow to the Pacific Ocean. Abundant sunshine nourished water plants such as widgeon-grass (Ruppia), pondweed (Patamogeton), smartweed (Polygonum), plus numerous species of algae.

It is impossible to estimate the untold millions of waterfowl which used this nourishing and protective region during primitive times. Waterfowl are so specialized in their feeding habits that they can inhabit the same marsh without competing each other into extinction. A zoologist once said that nature had to have ducks to hold a balance, and since there were none in Australia, it was necessary to invent the duckbilled platypus. Even today, it is possible to observe several species living together in the Klamath Basin National Wildlife refuges, some feeding on algae, some on leafy plants. Spoonbills may be screening the water for small crustaceans while their neighbors gather the material from the bottom. Graceful white swan stir the bottom with the advantage of a long neck, while the small birds wait patiently near them for a tidbit to float to the surface. In the same location pelicans and mergansers will be catching fish.

Pacific Flyway

The fortunate Modocs had another advantage working for them in the fact that the Sacramento Valley of California, prior to the development of dikes and water controls, provided a lush feeding ground for waterfowl. The climate of central California, so much different from the Klamath highland, was the natural stopping and wintering place for migratory birds after they left the Klamath country. This route has become known as the Pacific Flyway. The ancient people of Nightfire, not knowing that the migration routes were an ingrained instinct in the wildlife, probably credited the two annual bird migrations to the power and magic of the village shaman.

Of the migratory birds, among the first to arrive in the fall were the pintails and mallards. Among the last to show were the baldpate and canvasback. On the northward migration, the pintails and white snow geese again led the flights toward the north. The white-fronted geese, called "specks" by duck hunters, were among the last to arrive, usually in April.

On a normal winter season, most lakes and some streams freeze over but despite this, several bird species winter in these high basins. Jim O'Donahue, local naturalist, said that ruddy ducks, goldeneyes, buffleheads and a few mallards can be found in the open waters where the warm springs prevent the formation of ice. Swifter parts of streams also offer a winter feeding and resting place. The most noticeable winter-dwellers are the large Canada geese.

Coot, called mudhens locally, ordinarily travel south during the icy season, but a few hardy ones can be seen swimming and bobbing around in open waters. The common merganser, called fishduck, is sometimes found in the winter season.

Much of the former range of the Modocs is now included in three national wildlife refuges. The Clear Lake Refuge in Modoc County, California, includes 25,300 acres. The Tule Lake Refuge, California, contains 37,340 acres. The Lower Klamath Refuge, former home of the Nightfire Islanders, has 81,619 acres. At the time this refuge was established in 1908, one writer observed: "Literally clouds of birds of every species darkened the sky; the thunder of their wings was like the roar of the distant surf, and their voices drowned out all other sounds."

The numbers of birds have been reduced appreciably, but even so a survey made by the U.S. Department of Interior Fish and Wildlife Service in 1943 recorded 249 species on or near the refuges. The Modoc evidently ate few of the small birds but the potential selection of the larger species in the spring, summer and fall was great enough to assure that the storage baskets would be filled with dried ducks, and the bellies of the children would be provided with protein and calcium. For a list from the U.S. Fish and Wildlife Service which gives an idea of the different species available, see Supplement at end of book.

Bounty from the Nest

The survey shows that there are over forty species nesting in the Klamath region. The first to nest are the Canada geese, the big honkers which mate for life and start nesting in February. Other water birds follow later. Some duck families can be seen swimming about in midsummer, still small and downy. It is a wonder that they can fly by fall migration time.

To the Nightfire Islanders, the bird-nesting season was one of great joy. An egg cannot fly; it cannot sneak away; it does not bite and it has no fur or feathers to remove. A goose gives you eggs. When geese no longer leave eggs, ducks begin to leave eggs. What more could a hunting and gathering people want? The soils of Nightfire contained no eggs, but the value of the nesting birds in fulfilling the food cycle should not be underestimated.

Charlie Ogle, who grew up on the Klamath Indian Reservation, told of an invitation received by his father, Selden Ogle, to join a party of egg gatherers. After working from dugout canoes, they cooked a large number of the eggs in a wash boiler. While cracking and eating the eggs, Mr. Ogle noticed that many contained the developing birds. He tried to act nonchalant but his stomach was not as strong as his spirit. The Indians were greatly amused and said, "Whatamalla, Ogle, you no like young ducks?" Charlie said that the egg-gathering party really enjoyed the joke on his father.

Scientists Analyze the Modoc Diet

One of the purposes of Johnson's scientific team was to analyze the food habits of the Nightfire Islanders as much as possible from the types and numbers of mammal, fish and bird bones found in the soil of the excavated squares. In doing this, the work of another scientific field was called upon—that of geology. In the words of LeRoy Johnson:

"Dr. Laurence R. Kittleman, geologist, Museum of Natural History, University of Oregon, acts as soils-analyst without pay. He visited the site while excavations were underway and personally collected samples for his studies. Dr. Kittleman has done size-frequency analyses and a study of soil constituents. The resultant information will be useful for archaeologic interpretation since it will make it possible to segregate naturally deposited soils from midden accumulations in ambiguous cases, and to recognize specific natural events in the site's history. For example, Dr. Kittleman identified a deep horizon of volcanic pumice lapilli from the eruption of Mount Mazama, Oregon, that took place ca. 7,000 B.P., and which sets a maximum beginning date for the 4-SK-4 occupation." Fig. 30 shows Dr. Kittleman with an instrument used in determining the age of obsidian.

From the levels determined by the geologist, the bones could be identified within a time period. The brown paper sacks, so carefully marked at the time of excavation, were taken from storage. It then became the assignment of Donald Grayson to undertake

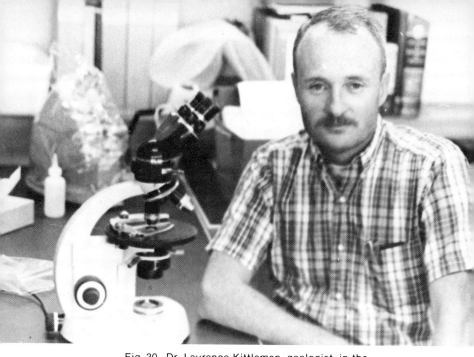

Fig. 30. Dr. Laurence Kittleman, geologist, in the
obsidian hydration laboratory.

Fig. 31. Dr. Donald Grayson
made analysis of bird and mammal bones.

the long, exacting job of examining and recording any information revealed by the thousands of bones. The first task was to determine the kind of animal they represented. In doing this, he worked closely with paleontologist, Arnold Shotwell. After species were identified, then counts of each species and the numbers in the different levels could be compared Fig. 31.

Grayson's careful and, no doubt, exhaustive study revealed that the contents of the brown paper sacks were exciting. For one thing, the great variety of birds eaten was surprising. Included were the usual coots, ducks, geese and swan, but also on the menu were the pelican, grebe, heron, cormorant, loon, plover, gull and merganser. While the bones of eagles, owls and ravens were discovered in the midden, the writer believes that they were captured for other purposes than for eating, although hunger may, at times, have changed the Modoc idea of what was edible.

Another finding from the bone study was the seasonal variety of the species found. For example, a pintail bird would suggest occupation of the site in the early spring or early fall. Perhaps the most revealing discovery resulting from Grayson's work was in finding the total numbers of birds and animals consumed during the various ages that the site was occupied. Since twenty carbon 14 tests of the charcoal in the various strata had been made, the seventeen levels of excavation were divided into five phases for the purposes of study. The eating habits then might be related to other factors in the Modoc environment, such as the water level of the lake, climate, or even hunting methods.

Since the carbon 14 dating was done on Nightfire Island, it has been discovered through the study of bristle-cone pine growth rings that a difference exists between carbon 14 years and actual calendar years. It is necessary to increase the scale of carbon 14 years on objects used before the Christian era. Such dates around 3,000 years Before Present should be increased by 200 calendar years. This becomes 800 years when increased to 7,000 years B.P. All dates given on Nightfire can be estimated accordingly, since the obsidian hydration has been based upon C 14 dates and correlated with it. Some scientists believe the variance in C 14 and calendar years was caused by sunspots. The accompanying chart, Fig. 32, shows the ages, soil types and dates of the levels studied.

Grayson found that in the first phase of occupation (7,000-5,000 B.P.) the bones of diving birds were most numerous. Coot, lesser and greater scaup dominated the count, with dabbling ducks and geese far below in percentages. This continued through the second phase and early into the beginning of the third. Then about 4,000 B.P., the numbers of ducks and geese consumed made a marked increase, while the diving ducks showed an equally marked decrease. Coot consumption stayed about the same until around 2,000 years B.P. and then went down. The numbers of surface-feeding birds remained high into the fifth and last phase. From this Grayson reasoned that the lake must have been deeper during the time the first formations of the island were laid down, about 7,000-3,500 B.P., since this deep-water condition would have created a favorable habitat for the diving birds. His proposal was qualified by the following statement: "Each of these statements must be considered a hypothesis to be tested on the basis of pertinent available data."

Since his study, other data has become available and it is likely that if Dr. Grayson had been able to take part in the excavation, he might have arrived at a different hypothesis in this case. The lakebed sediments on which the island was built would have been under six feet of water had the lake been deep. However, the findings from the bone studies may be even more revealing than first imagined when the dissertation was completed. Dr. Grayson's study, now an unpublished doctoral dissertation, has proved to be a valuable permanent contribution to the knowledge of Indian food habits. The data from the birds, when matched in developments in hunting methods and projectile points, is indeed interesting.

Age of the Bolas

After an examination of this data, Linda Verrett noted, "There seems to be a jump in the number of small, stemmed and corner-notched arrowheads at level 7, phase 3 (about 2,500 years B.P.)

PHASE	LEVEL	SOIL TYPE	STRUCTURE	EARLIEST C14 DATE	LATEST C14 DATE	EARLIEST OBSIDIAN DATE	LATEST OBSIDIAN DATE	
5	1	ORGANIC LOAM						SHOSHONEAN
5	2	ORGANIC LOAM						
4	3	HARD PAN						GUNTHER POINTS
4	4	HARD PAN		2080	930	2885	721	DABBLING DUCKS
4	5	HARD PAN						
4	6	HARD PAN						
3	7	BROWN + BLACK LOAM						BISON ⎫ DISAPPEAR
3	8	BROWN + BLACK LOAM		4150	2180	3869	1490	WOLF ⎭
3	9	BROWN + BLACK LOAM						GEESE INCREASE
3	10	BROWN + BLACK LOAM						
2	11	BLACK BAND		4750BP	4380	7663	3651	DIVING DUCKS
2	12	BLACK BAND						COOT DOMINATE
1	13	SAND		6080BP	5150BP	7327BP	56518P	
1	14	DUCK MUCK						
1	15	DUCK MUCK						
1	16	DUCK MUCK						
	17	STERILE CLAY WITH DIATOMS — PUMICE						

Fig. 32. Ages, soil types and dates of levels studied.

Fig. 33. Numerous football-shaped bolas stones were concentrated in the yellow duck-muck layer.

Fig. 34. Some biconical stones were too crudely made for gaming stones.

Fig. 35. Round "duck balls" were used with a sling near Lakeport, California. Flat skipping stones called "duck rocks" were numerous on some waterfowl sites.

that corresponds to the beginning of the peak in the dabbling duck remains." LeRoy Johnson made another significant observation that relates to the dabbling ducks when he stated that the small, football-shaped stones, formerly called gaming stones, seem to have gone out of use about this same date. He further observed that this could have been the time of the invention or introduction of the bow and arrow.

It seems logical, yet amazing, to find evidence that the date for the invention or introduction of the bow in the Klamath region corresponds closely with its adoption in Lovelock Cave, Nevada. Cressman said that the bow replaced the atlatl about 2,300 years ago at that site.

Could the Modocs have used the bolas for taking birds? The answer is obviously yes. The entire island is underlaid with these small stones. Some were found on the white lakebed soil, others in the yellow, duck-stained sand above the lakebed. The stones, quite numerous before 3,500 B.P., suddenly disappear in the upper levels of the island. In one square of approximately 2 meters, 54 of these stones, Fig. 33, were found embedded in the duck-stained sand. The spot must once have been an open pothole in the marsh vegetation where the primitive hunters could sneak up on the waterfowl and entangle them in their bolas. Any occasional losses over the years could result in the numerous stones found in the area.

The widespread use of the bolas is further confirmed by the fact that virtually every square meter of the island contained one or more bolas stones, some crudely made as in Fig. 34. They were always found in the lower strata of the island.

Another guided missile stone, which was used prior to and probably after the introduction of the bow and arrow, is the simple, flat skipping-rock. These are called by some Paiutes "duck rocks." Those at the lower half in Fig. 35 are typical. Their use at Nightfire was limited but there are thousands of them near the shores of Crump Lake in Lake County, Oregon, and to a lesser extent around other playa lakes in Warner Valley. All have been shaped by the Indians into generally square forms. Some have slight side-notches as though attached together in the manner of a bolas set.

A third type of missile found abundantly on the wind-blown, dry bed of Crump Lake is indicated by water-washed rocks slightly larger than walnuts. It is plain that they were carefully selected for size and shape, although there is no sign that shaping or work was done on them by Indians. The author believes that the rounded rocks were thrown with a sling. One argument against this is that they are frequently discovered in groups of six to ten as though they had been used on a net or bolas.

Duck Balls of the Pomo

A type of missile that was certainly used with a sling is the clay balls in the upper half of Fig. 35. During the drought of 1976-1977, the waters of Clear Lake in Lake County, California, lowered to the point where the bottom of the lake was exposed. Baked clay balls, called duck balls, were found in abundance where the Pomos or their ancestors had thrown them at waterfowl. There has been no evidence of clay duck balls in the realm of the Modoc or Northern Paiute.

The Atlatl

It seems a little strange to think of hunting anything as small as a duck with an atlatl-thrown dart. First, the problem of accuracy seems overwhelming. Then the distance factor adds to the difficulty of the hunter. Yet, projectile points of the early-period strata, heavily mixed with duck bones, strongly indicates that the pioneer hunters used the atlatl, Fig. 36. Certainly the bow and arrow had not been invented at this stage. An argument against the atlatl presence at Nightfire is the fact that no single fragment of an atlatl weight has been found in the strata there.

In the Cradle Culture at Clear Lake, the slender cigar-shaped weights were found along with other features characteristic of early man. The atlatl weights shown in Fig. 37 were certainly a part of the heritage handed to the Nightfire Modoc. The atlatl

Fig. 36. Large side-notched points were used before the bow and arrow.

Fig. 37. Atlatl weights from the Cradle Culture had gone out of style before Nightfire was occupied.

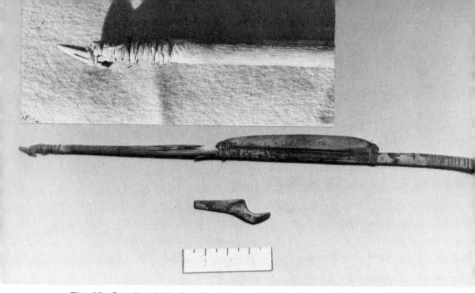

Fig. 38. Small atlatl showing the weight in place with large atlatl hook below. (Favell Museum)

Fig. 39. Unusual atlatl weight that was fastened through a hole in the center.

from Nevada, now in the Favell Museum in Klamath Falls, Fig. 38, shows how the weight was placed on the throwing stick. The purpose of the weight is not known but the dart to be thrown was engaged in the hook at the end of the atlatl opposite the handle. The device provided an extension of the human arm, giving the dart greater velocity.

If no atlatl weights were found at Nightfire Island, how could the hunters have used the atlatl? Evidence seems to indicate that the weights had simply gone out of style. Perhaps the stones had no real purpose except to bring the thrower good luck. Certainly the atlatl weight was known to the Lower Klamath Modoc. The one shown in Fig. 39 was found on Sheepy Ridge by Andy McKay. It is different from others in that a hole was bored through it to provide an attachment to the handle. Most weights have been attached by means of a groove cut in one or both ends to hold the sinew. Another fragment found on the Langer Ranch shows that it was probably used centuries before the first Modocs moved to Nightfire Island.

The small size of some of the projectile points in the lower strata makes one wonder how they could possibly have been used on an atlatl dart, especially on waterfowl. An answer was found in the words of Justin Locke, who wrote on the "Lost Kingdom in Indian Mexico" (Oct. 1952) in the *National Geographic Magazine*: "To the right a lonely boatman was hunting coots and ducks from his canoe. With scarcely a ripple, his boat slid through a thousand tiny dots. Slowly the boatman rose and threw his long spear, or fisga, in a high arc. With a flashing of wings the birds whirred into the air. But the hunter had made his kill. To launch his fisga, he had used a spear thrower, or atlatl, which provides a catapultic action. Tata Pedro assured me that this weapon, an earlier development than the bow, is effective up to 150 feet."

It now appears that many more unweighted throwing sticks were used than weighted ones. The limited numbers of these stones found even in old material cultures led to the belief that they were unusual rather than common. The small size of the

Favell Museum atlatl from Nevada shows that some atlatl darts were probably no heavier than the arrows later used with bows.

Food was not the only thing the migrating millions of waterfowl brought to the Modoc. Their feathers served for decorations and for the guiding vanes on the arrows. Even of greater importance were the downy feathers that gave protection in the winter weather. The bird skins were cut into strips, then twisted so that the feathers extended on all sides of the skin cordage. These were then woven into blankets and robes in the same way the Paiute of the Great Basin wove rabbit-skin blankets. The first to observe this type of dress was Peter Skene Ogden, who led the Hudson's Bay Company party through the Modoc country in 1827.

Special permission from the Smithsonian Institution has been granted to publish the picture of a birdskin blanket shown in Fig. 40.

Processing Waterfowl Meat

During the two seasons each year when the waterfowl passed through the Sheepy Creek region, the problem of supplying provisions was simple—fresh meat or eggs for each meal. To provide food in the off season, a method had to be developed to preserve the meat without refrigeration or salt. One old-time cowboy in the region told the author that he had seen the Modocs clubbing young birds, dressing them, then hanging them on willow racks to dry. The windy plateau country was ideal for drying the dressed waterfowl. Getting the hard, dry carcasses into an edible condition was another problem. The author believes that the large stone mortars provided the method of grinding the birds into a mixture of powdered meat mixed with the calcium of the powdered bone.

Anywhere in the Klamath country where rock ledges are available adjacent to the marshes, there are also usually found bedrock mortars as pictured in Fig. 41. Such mortars probably served as community property available when not already in use. Multiple bedrock mortars indicate they may have been a primitive "sewing circle" type operation. In the case of Nightfire Island, there were

Fig. 40. Modoc feather blanket. (Smithsonian Institution permit no. 77-11-310)

only the rocks carried by the inhabitants. Large mortars and fragments of mortars, such as those in Fig. 42, took the place of the
bedrock type. Such bowls are common but not all of them are as
well shaped as the big ones pictured. Most of the larger ones were
pointed on the bottom so that they could be set into the soil while
in use. Some were beautifully shaped; others appeared to be simple rocks with a hole ground out to fit the pestle.

Manufacture of Stone Implements

Considering the size of the mortars and the tools available to
the Indian women who made them, it would seem that a lifetime
would be required for the manufacture of a single mortar. The
main tool required in making a mortar would be a type of ham-
merstone, normally just a hand-sized rock, a little harder than the
stone to be processed. The stones in the bottom of Fig. 43 are called "hard rocks." They have not been shaped as hammerstones in
the finished way that flaking stones are made. They are simply
rocks of a dense material capable of holding up under repeated
hammering. The stones in the upper part of the figure are abrasive and of coarse, volcanic material. They have been used to
shape and smooth other objects of wood, stone or antler.

By striking blow after blow with a hard rock, a few grains of
sand would fall away and the shape would gradually emerge.
Sometimes the women shaped the outside of the bowl first, then
started to work the inside. The maker of the mortar shown in Fig.
44 used this method. She evidently had pecked a ring around,
leaving a center to be broken out later. After a sufficient hollow
was established for the use of the pestle, the grinding of food
could begin. Normal use of the pestle would then deepen the hole,
increasing the grinding surface. Eventually the bowl would wear
entirely through. Great patience must have been required to stay
with a job long enough to finish a stone mortar.

Most large mortars were made of vesicular lava but many small
ones, like those in Fig. 45, were of a much lighter and more
porous volcanic material.

Fig. 41. Large bedrock mortar on Fish and Wildlife Reserve.

Fig. 42. Giant Nightfire mortars with pestles. (The white tag is 4 inches long.)

Fig. 43. "Hard rocks" were more dense to withstand hammering. Upper row contains porous stones for use as a rasp or as sandpaper.

Fig. 44. This large mortar was started by pecking a ring inside with hard rocks.

The inside of the Modoc mortar almost always had a pointed bottom made by the circular motion of the grinding process used to pulverize meat, Fig. 46. This shape is quite different from that used by most California tribes, where acorns provided a large part of the diet. The mortar can almost be used as a diagnostic tool in establishing the boundary between the territory of the Modoc and the Shasta. The Shastas in Siskiyou County, California, settled for the acorn and salmon—the Modoc for waterfowl, suckers and the ipo.

For a tribe whose livelihood depended so much on birds, the coming of the bow and arrow must have been a dramatic event. To those who had depended upon the hand-thrown spear, or the forceful but clumsy atlatl, the new invention would have meant more change than the invention of nuclear fission. The bolas was effective in capturing waterfowl, but the range was limited to the distance that a man could throw the football-shaped stones. There is no way of telling exactly when the bow came to the Modocs, nor is there any way to determine whether it was invented by their own Thomas Edison, or if it was carried to the village by a traveler from another tribe.

New Projectile Point

The bow and arrow is said to have been introduced to the basket-maker people in Arizona about the year 400 A.D. Certainly the bow was used by the Nightfire Islanders long before this. A bow fragment was found in Cougar Mountain Cave by Cowles, which was said to be about 1200 to 1600 years old.

Several things occurred in the lives of those dwelling on Sheepy Creek during the centuries around 3500 years ago. The bolas stones so abundantly scattered among the rocks and bones of the village disappeared. The waterfowl diet, which had included mostly birds of the diving species, began to change to include much larger numbers of the dabbling ducks, which were also better fliers than the diving ducks.

Another change, even easier to detect, was that made in the type of weapons. The projectile points which had shown a pre-

Fig. 45. Lighter volcanic stone was used for these small mortars.

Fig. 46. Broken mortars show the typical pointed-shape bottom
made by the Modoc.

ponderance of side-notched and corner-notched types shifted to a new, lighter fashion. One of these had a single stem and is now called a Gunther Point.

Why were the hunters willing to give up the heavier side-notched arrows that had served them so well for 4000 years? Probably for two reasons: first, archaeological evidence found by Cressman and others supports the fact that the Modoc bow was quite light and rather small. It is true that by historic times the larger and better bows from neighboring tribes had been traded into the area of the lake-dwelling people. No such large bows have been found, however, in circumstances that indicated much antiquity. The bow, and the fragments of the bow, shown in Fig. 47, are both prehistoric, and fit into the same pattern as those age-dated bows found in caves. The longer one was preserved in the mucky bottom of the Klamath River; the other was pulled from a tule bank where the tannic acid of the marsh had preserved it. If a light bow (nteyaga) were to be used, then a light arrowpoint was needed to go with the lesser amount of propulsion.

The second reason for a change in the style of arrows was the type of material available for arrowshafts. There is no doubt that the stems of cattails (widshibam) were used for shafts. The favored arrowshaft was more probably made from the bamboo-like cane grass called *Phragmites phragmites*. Both were light and abundant and right at the site where the arrowmakers lived. The single small end of the obsidian arrow would fit into the end of the arrowshaft where it could be bound with sinew.

The marsh-dwelling Modocs and Klamaths used many more arrowpoints made of wood than obsidian. In 1880 A.D., Modocs called the obsidian points "war arrows" (npeisll), although few of the thousands they made were ever used for war. These obsidian points were sometimes attached to a wooden foreshaft which was then attached to the cane arrowshaft. For waterfowl, the wooden arrowheads, sometimes surrounded by a ring of pitch, were made so that they would skip along the water and into a flock of birds. The remains of the wooden arrowpoints have long since disappeared except where they were deposited in dry caves.

Fig. 47. Small bows were used prior to contact with Europeans.

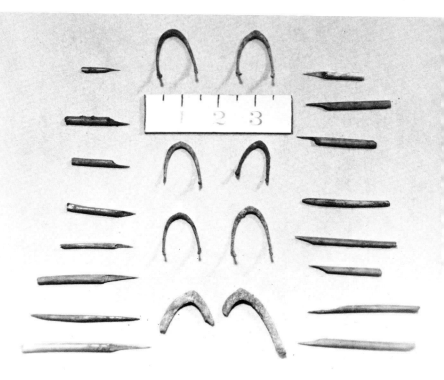

Fig. 48. Birdbone arrowpoints with waterfowl breastbones.

Another type of point, perhaps the one that served as a pattern for those made of wood, was found in one part of Nightfire Island. These were made of birdbone, Fig. 48, shown with the breast bones of waterfowl. They were ideally suited for mounting on a cane shaft. They could also easily be fitted with the pitch ring necessary for water skipping. This might be one reason that the dabbling ducks increased in the percentage of bones found by Dr. Grayson.

The skilled arrowmakers were so good at making side-notched arrows that it seems they would have developed the Shoshonean or desert side-notched type. This was not destined to occur until much later. It was not until about 1450 A.D. that the small and delicate Shoshonean points would become popular with both Klamath and Modoc.

If the bow and arrow brought bad news to the dabbling ducks, the small mammals were given little relief by the invention. Among the numbers of bones found in the fourth phase of occupation, a marked increase was found in rabbits, ground squirrels and small carnivorous animals such as otter. Even a few fat beaver appeared on the menu at this period.

End of the Bolas

The disappearance of the football-shaped bolas stones near the end of the second phase, about 3500 years ago, did not mean the discontinuance in use of small stones by the Modocs. About three types of such stones were used. The author can offer no substantial evidence concerning the purpose for which they were used. One such type, the small cylindrical stones shown in Fig. 49, at right, have had a band cut around them to hold a cord or sinew thong. The entire cache of 34 was found together, indicating that they were likely used on a single device. There is no way of knowing for sure if they were used on a fish net, a bolas, or perhaps a super-bolas. The small stones may have been part of a net cast to entrap sitting or flying birds.

Another type of stone was found in caches or groups ranging from three to twenty-seven and is shown in Fig. 49. These are crudely made, or perhaps they were not made at all, just selected for size. The shape is similar to the earlier, carefully made bolas stones, but they are not as well made nor are they water-washed pebbles like those found at Crump Lake.

The third type of stones, for which no purpose can be offered, is the single pebbles which have been slightly notched to hold a sinew cord or buckskin. On some sites they would be considered fish-line weights or fish-net weights. At Nightfire they were found in all phases and singly rather than in groups. Perhaps they should simply be called "notched pebbles" and each reader be allowed to figure out their purpose.

When the founders of Nightfire first moved to the site, they had to travel down the creek to reach the then-existing marsh. Most waterfowl are extremely cautious. Ducks will fly over an area three or four times before gliding in for a landing. Canada geese are among the most intelligent of birds. How could the anxious hunters get enough birds within range of their bolas sets or atlatls to supply the village? They must have developed many ways of attracting and stalking the various kinds of waterfowl. They obviously knew the use of decoys as this method has great antiquity. See the picture taken in the Nevada Historical Society Museum in Reno, Nevada, Fig. 50. These decoys were discovered in an ancient cave. They are made of duckskins stuffed with tules.

Bone game-calls such as those in Figs. 51 and 52 were also used. These, all from Nightfire, differ from multiple-note whistles sometimes used by the Klamath Indians. To get a tone from the bone game-call, the hunter placed his lips on the hole, then made noise by sucking on the bone rather than blowing as with a trumpet. The broken tube at the bottom of the figure is the only true whistle found on the island. It is made of mammal bone.

It would have been interesting to see the hunter with his canoe or balsa raft hidden in the cattails with either bolas or atlatl ready. With the great flocks of waterfowl overhead, he should not have had to wait long before the decoys or game-calls brought the birds within range. Then a silent movement and breakfast would soon be ready.

Fig. 49. Stones, at left, were unaltered. Those, at right, were shaped to hold cordage.

Fig. 50. Ancient decoys from a Nevada cave. (Nevada Historical Society)

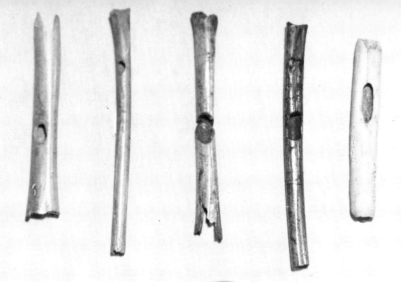

Fig. 51. Game calls used by the Modoc were not true whistles.

Fig. 52. Longer birdbone objects with perforations for use as flutes.

Those who built a lifestyle based on waterfowl made traps and nets to capture birds. The Northwest Indians developed a technique in which a net was laid on the ground near a waterhole used by the birds. They were captured by having one person frighten the ducks into rapid flight while others raised the net between the poles to entrap the birds. Cressman said that Klamath Indians devised a way of catching ducks in a net stretched between two canoes. In the late evening after dusk, or in the early morning, the waterfowl were scared into the waiting nets. The stones in Fig. 49 are about the right size for such a net weight. All appeared in phase-four levels, long after the bolas stones had gone out of use.

4. ANIMAL FOODS OF THE MODOC

Cooking Large Mammals

The building of Nightfire Island was done without architect or plan, without intention or even purpose. The island was built primarily because of the skill of the hunters. Small animals and plants could be boiled in baskets. The cooking of large animals required longer heating and larger rocks. So the islanders built each day, year, and century as they cooked and ate.

When the move was made to the creek bank, the weapons for big-game hunting had already been developed. Likewise, the cooking methods were established from an earlier phase. The job of carrying the stones seems overwhelming when viewed today, but one cooking oven might last a generation. As the generations passed, the island rose in height.

Roasting ovens contain mostly plain basalt rocks, some as large as one person can lift. Mixed with them are broken fragments of mortars, pestles and an exceptionally large number of banded stones used for weights, Fig. 53. Weighing from 8 to 18 pounds, some are so crudely made that it is hard to see the bands or notches used for the attachment of cordage. In the past they have been generally called canoe anchors by those who found them. At Nightfire the location on the house floors and in the roasting pits leads to the belief that they served as weights to hold the house matting or rafters in place.

Fig. 53. Large stone weights were often found in cooking ovens.

Fig. 54. Hides were stretched
before tanning.

Fig. 55. Old people's mortars could be carried.

Fig. 56. Small mortars were often irregular in shape.

Another use, suggested by Dave Cole, was that they could have been used for hide stretchers as shown in Fig. 54. The stones are much heavier than necessary for anchors on the dugout canoes. Also they seem more numerous than would be expected for canoe anchors, or even as weights for the balsa-type rafts used by the Modocs.

Most stones in the roasting platforms show signs of burning and are intermingled with the charcoal of the cooking fires. The stones seem purposely fitted together. It is possible that they could have been placed on a house floor. However, since so much of the site is underlaid with rocks, it is probable that outdoor cooking was practiced.

Old People's Mortar

Another method of cooking that was popular was that of boiling food in a basket. Stones were heated, then dropped into a tightly woven basket containing water and left until the heat was dissipated. The operation was then repeated until the contents reached the required edible state. Apparently rocks used for basketry cooking were not shaped to any particular form, otherwise the midden would contain many such stones. For boiling food, apparently any basalt or lava rock the desired size to convey heat was used. The rocks were lifted from the fire with wooden tongs and placed in the cooking basket.

The bubbling food, without doubt, contained ash from the fire and fragments from heated stones, since the teeth of the islanders became worn at an early age. Their dental problems must have been painful—even too severe for the songs of the shaman to cure. The Modocs did provide one technique to reduce the pain of toothache and made ash-laden food more digestible—the old people's mortar, Fig. 55. It was light enough to carry, and it was used to give food a secondary grinding. These small stone bowls enabled the aged to chew after their teeth were worn off. Not all such mortars were well shaped; most were simply a stone, usually porous in nature, that had a bowl ground in one side like those in Fig. 56.

Modoc mythology mentions another feature of the way old people, whose teeth were gone, adapted to the foods available. Roasted liver was called "old people's food." This was evidently an accepted and generous concession to the aged when choices in foods were limited.

American Bison

The objects of the hunt killed by the islanders have proved to be amazing. Perhaps the most unusual animal discovery was the bones of the American buffalo (*Bison bison*) which were found in each of the first three phases of occupation. It was the first evidence that these animals had lived in this part of California and Oregon. Very probably, during this period the flat bed of Lower Klamath Lake was a grassy plain similar to the previous postglacial period when the area was inhabited by the camel. In any case, Grayson found roasted buffalo was on the menu from 7,000 B.P. until about 3,000 B.P. and then disappeared.

Although the buffalo disappeared from the Klamath country about 3,000 years ago, there was a word in the Lutuami language for the animal. This word has an interesting connection with the official name of a Paiute band of Indians. Selden Kirk was long recognized as tribal leader and head of the Klamath-Modoc-Paiute tribal council. It is fortunate that Van Landrum was able to spend many hours visiting with the old Indian prior to his death. One interesting observation made by Landrum was in the derivation of the word "yahooskin," used when the treaty was signed with the Paiute band by the United States government. The word "yoho" was the Klamath Indian name for buffalo and was pronounced by Mr. Kirk as "you hoe." Ckne or ckni means "people from" thus yuho ckne would be "people from the buffalo country" or "buffalo people." It follows that the word was corrupted to be spelled and pronounced yahooskin to designate the Snake band occupying the region of Beatty at the time the Klamath Indian Reservation was established in 1864. It would be hard to determine actually how far away the nearest living buffalo would have been then, probably in Idaho or Nevada.

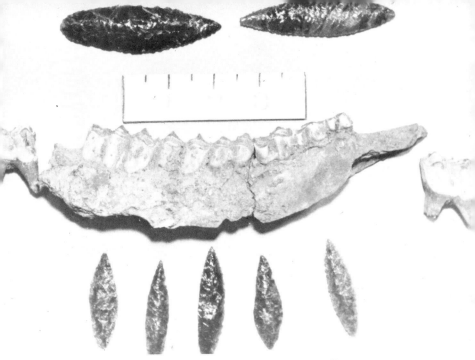

Fig. 57. Cascade-type points were among the earliest.

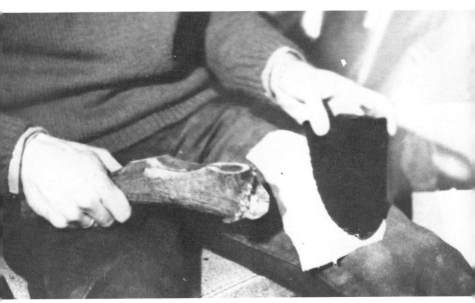

Fig. 58. Deer antler provided one type of percussion flaker.

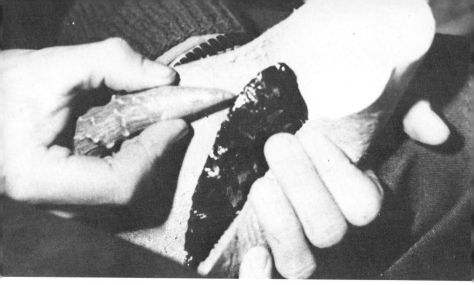

Fig. 59. The point of an antler was used for percussion flaking.

Fig. 60. Pressure flakers with a variety of type points.

Usually buffalo hunters are pictured on horses riding alongside the ponderous beasts with a drawn bow or hand-held spear. Of course, the braves of Nightfire had no horses and the bow would not be invented for two or three thousand years. As the thick hides of the buffalo were hard to penetrate, a strong propulsion was required. Without doubt, the atlatl dart was used and a sharp, heavy projectile point was needed to bring down the animals either with atlatl or hand-held spear.

Throughout the thousands of years that the hunters ranged the hills adjacent to their island, the favorite material for making these projectile points was obsidian. This is often called volcanic glass and, except for certain impurities, it is very much like ordinary glass. It seems impossible that one volcano can issue such a variety of stone materials as pumice, scoria, lava, and the shiny obsidian. The reason obsidian is so different from the other volcanic materials is that it is cooler at the time of eruption, usually about 600 to 850 degrees centigrade. As a result, the surface of the silica rapidly chills, causing it to harden into a jell before it has time to crystallize. It usually forms in colors of gray, translucent black, or grainy black, sometimes in a mixture of red and black, rarely in blue or green.

Working of Obsidian

Fortunately for the arrowmakers, obsidian also has other qualities which make it desirable for use in weapons. The points shown with the teeth of the bison in Fig. 57 are called Cascade-type points. They are one of the three most common types found in the earliest levels of the ancient camp. It seems impossible that material as fragile as volcanic glass could be shaped accurately by the primitive craftsmen.

Bruce Bradley of Tucson, Arizona, has, over the years, practiced duplicating the work of ancient knapping artists. He has been called upon to demonstrate at universities and analyze the techniques found in archaeological sites. He first selects an obsidian block, then, holding it on one knee, he strikes the upper edge with a rock called a percussion flaker, Fig. 58. The spalls are

struck with either rocks or antlers. There is some waste but carefully struck spalls seem to come off the core in about the same
thickness. After spalls are struck, Bradley demonstrates two different methods for shaping the material into the size and style
desired. One method, percussion, produces wider, shorter flakes,
whether done with a stone or antler hammer. The pressure technique, Fig. 59, brings a narrower, longer flake and enables the
maker to exercise better control of the material. Ancient arrowmakers used both percussion and pressure flaking. Fig. 60 shows
several pressure-flaking tools made of bone and antler used by the
artisans of Nightfire, along with some of the more unusual shaped
projectile points in use before the bow and arrow. In order to
illustrate the difference in appearance of the two types of flakes,
Bradley made a blade with the short, wide percussion flakes on
one side and the longer, narrower pressure flakes on the other
side, Fig. 61.

The amount of control that a skilled workman can exercise over
obsidian is amazing. Theodore Orcutt, a Karok Indian, once lived at Red Rock near Dorris, California. He learned the arrow-
maker's art from his father, who was the village specialist. The
giant blade, Fig. 62, now in the Nevada Historical Museum at
Reno, Nevada, is an example of his work, though not ancient, it
represents the almost lost heritage of an ancient art. Orcutt told
Alfred Collier of Klamath Falls that it took years of practice for
him to become proficient.

The men who did the knapping at Nightfire village apparently
used a stone anvil to hold the obsidian being worked. These stones
always have a small pit worn into one side and sometimes on both
sides. Most of the anvils in Fig. 63 have also been used as hammerstones to break the spalls from the obsidian block. They were
then used to hold the spalls for further percussion work. Anvils
have been so numerous that there is reason to believe they must
have been employed for other purposes than knapping, perhaps
for cracking bones. The narrow diameter of the worn pit rules out
their use with a maul for pounding food.

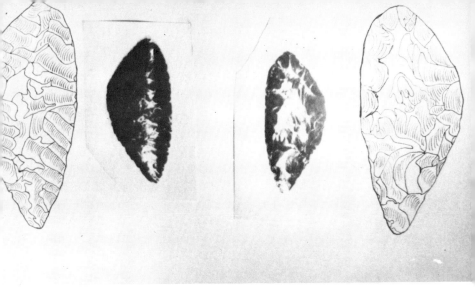

Fig. 61. Pressure flakes at left, wider percussion flakes at right.

Fig. 62. Nevada Historical Society blade of Glass Mountain obsidian.

Fig. 63. Anvil rocks and hammer stones.

Fig. 64. Reject-spalls are still found along the edge of Glass Mountain.

Sources of Obsidian

Obsidian had great value to the Modoc arrowmakers, but it has other qualities which make it useful to researchers studying the habits of the Indians. One of these qualities, according to the scientists, is that obsidian is a homogenous mixture with abundant trace elements. Units of glass can be typed or fingerprinted. Each occurrence, be it flow or float, has its own chemical trademark. This can be discovered by a process called instrumental neutron activation analysis. The samples from Nightfire were irradiated in the Trica reactor at Reed College in Portland, Oregon.

In order to find where the Nightfire Modocs obtained their obsidian, sources in Northern California and adjacent areas in Oregon were explored and samples were collected from twenty-nine of these, including a few in Idaho and Nevada. After the chemical identity of each source was determined, 108 samples from the various levels excavated were then tested to determine the point where the ancient knappers obtained their material. The sources of all but three of the 108 samples were found.

The most popular source was from Glass Mountain, which lies south of the Lava Beds National Monument about 18 miles distant. This great obsidian flow has been the result of a series of volcanic events. The black, shiny blocks, Fig. 64, still show where travelers from various tribes have come to chip off pieces that could be carried home. Fragments of reject spalls are still found in the workshops near the flow. A surprising discovery was that 24 of the specimens studied were carried from Buck Mountain near Eagleville, California. This flow is more than twice as far away as Glass Mountain or Tucker Butte, which was the source of only one specimen. The map in Fig. 65 shows the trails and distances traveled to various sources.

There have been several theories to account for the willingness of the Modocs to travel such a distance for chipping material when a closer source was available. The first theory is that the arrowmakers, usually old men, simply liked the obsidian from Buck

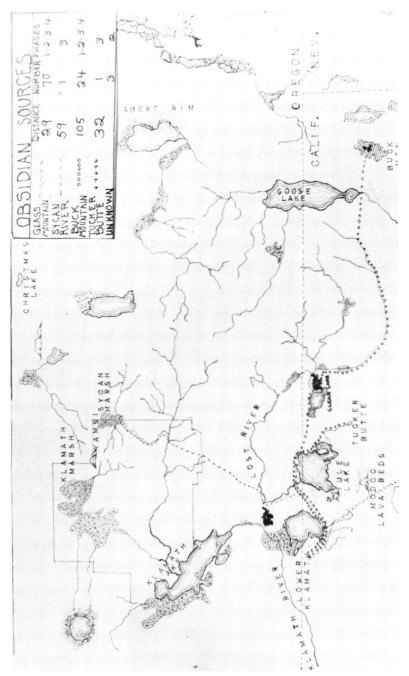

Fig. 65. Obsidian Trails.

Mountain so much better that they were willing to travel the extra distance to get it, even with the added risk of entering the territory of the Paiute and Pit River Indians.

Dr. David Easterla, of Western Missouri University, suggested that other tribes or enemy bands of Modocs may have held possession of the obsidian flows during certain time periods, thus effectively keeping the Nightfire arrow-knappers from the source at Glass Mountain. A third theory, and probably the most plausible, was suggested by Mac Heebner, Ranger Naturalist at Modoc Lava Beds National Monument. He suggests that there were periods of intense volcanic activity occurring during the 7000-year history of the Nightfire people, the most recent only 650 years ago. During these periods, the glass flows of the Medicine Lake volcano were simply too hot to go near and the fear of the mountain spirits was too fresh in the minds of the obsidian gatherers.

Obsidian Hydration and Dating

Obsidian has still another quality that makes it valuable for research—it absorbs water at a fixed rate. In looking at the hard, glassy surface of obsidian, it seems unbelievable that its surface could be penetrated by water. The fact is that it can be penetrated and will absorb water. This makes it additionally valuable as a research tool which can be used to discover the age of the ancient people of the Klamath country. Obsidian in a given region with a similar climate, including temperature, rainfull and altitude, will absorb water at about the same rate. The age of the obsidian can be determined by measuring the depth that moisture has penetrated the surface. For the measurement to be accurate, a very complex procedure must be followed to establish an obsidian hydration rate.

It was in this accomplishment that Dr. LeRoy Johnson's research made a lasting contribution to the field of science, and especially to the future study of the Siskiyou, Modoc and Klamath area of California and Oregon. Before obsidian can be used for dating, the site must have the more conventional carbon 14 tests made. For the Nightfire site, the carbon dates were established by

Dr. K. Kigoshi, of Gakushuin University in Japan. Following this, Johnson set about developing the formula for an obsidian hydration rate, as it is called. *Science Magazine*, Sept. 26, 1969, published Johnson's report. Excerpts from his report describe the procedure:

"An obsidian-hydration rate of $3.5_4u^2/10^3$ radiocarbon years has been established for the Klamath Basin of California and Oregon. The study was conducted as a part of the Nightfire Island Project (1) of the University of Oregon's Museum of Natural History. The new rate provides a means to date prehistoric Klamath Basin obsidian-chipping and habitation sites in terms of their radiocarbon age. It will be an important adjunct to local archaeology, for natural glass is the chief source of artifact stone.

"In brief, obsidian dating works this way: When natural glass is fractured during the manufacture of artifacts such as knives or projectile points, freshly exposed surfaces are provided on the chipping flakes and the finished specimens. These surfaces take up ambient water to form a hydrated surface layer different in its density and refractive index from the remainder of the obsidian. Chemical composition of the obsidian and temperature are two factors that control the rate of hydration (3,5), and the thickness of the hydrated layer, then, depends upon time, temperature, and chemical composition. This section of each specimen is cut normal to the hydration layer and the layer thickness is measured under magnification using transmitted light.

"To calculate local rates of hydration for obsidians of different chemical compositions occurring in different climatic regions, correlations are made between a large number of obsidian measurements and contextually associated C^{14} age determinations in each area.

"Sometime after the climatic eruption of Mt. Mazama, Oregon (6), now dated at 7000 radiocarbon years B.P. (7), much of Lower Klamath Lake either drained or dried, and the forebears of the historic Modoc Indians moved onto the margins of the dry lake bed and began using the site as a habitation, fishing, and

duck-hunting station. The occupation dates from about 6000 to
500 radiocarbon years B.P. The Nightfire Island sequence of
projectile-point styles is the most complete and best stratified sequence available for the Klamath Basin. This fact, along with the
rather complete series of C 14 dates, makes the site ideal for the
establishment of an obsidian hydration rate. Nightfire Island will
serve as a reference site for local archaeology, for cross dating and
correlating the many Klamath Basin sites that represent briefer
occupations.

"Since the rate of hydration is dependent on temperature, a
given rate is applicable only to the climatic zone where it was
established. The present hydration rate applies, then, to the
Klamath Basin which includes Upper Klamath Lake, the Lost
River drainage, Lower Klamath Lake, and Tule Lake.

"It would be unwise to attempt to use the Klamath Basin rate
in any precise way outside this local region. The Great Basin proper, to the east, has higher temperatures. The Cascade Mountains, to the west, and the mountainous California highlands, to
the south, are colder. A possible exception is that part of the
Oregon Great Basin where the towns of Burns and Bend are
located. These weather stations represent a climatic belt which
parallels the northern margin of the Great Basin where the cli-
matological data are similar to those of the Klamath Basin. The
interior parts of the Great Basin, because of higher temperatures,
should yield a slightly greater hydration rate than the Klamath
Basin."

From the carbon 14 dates established at Gakushuin University,
the earliest date found in each phase has been recorded in the
fifth column of the chart on Fig. 32 of the previous chapter. The
latest carbon 14 date is entered in the sixth column. From the
many obsidian dates found by Johnson, the earliest date is recorded in the seventh column and the latest date in the eighth
column.

Neither carbon nor obsidian dates can be considered exact as
there must be a tolerance for a margin of error. In the case of obsidian dates, it is especially important not to rely upon a single

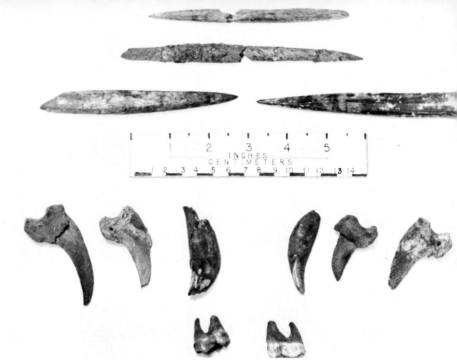

Fig. 66. Large bone points with bear bones.

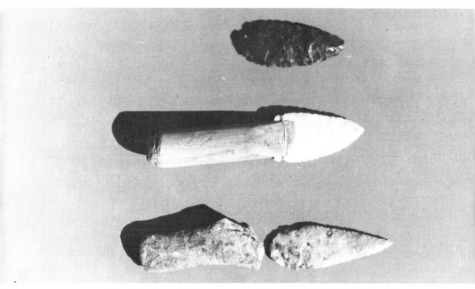

Fig. 67. Some knives were notched and fitted with handles.

specimen as Indians sometimes found older artifacts and used them along with those of their own manufacture. The dating of the various phases has also provided valuable information about the animals that once lived in the Modoc homeland.

Giant Grizzly

If finding the meat of the buffalo on the menu of the Modoc seems a spectacular discovery, it certainly was not the most dangerous animal to those who did the hunting. The bones and teeth of the giant California grizzly bear was another now extinct animal that challenged the courage and skill of the Nightfire braves. We may never know their method of taking these great beasts but in the sands and cooking ovens of the camp there is a common association of the bone points with the remains of wolf, bear and coyote. Could these bone points have been the darts that carried poison?

There is no archaeological evidence of the use of the poisoned arrow or dart. In the Modoc language, however, there is such evidence. The phrase "stetmash ngesh" means poisoned arrow, although the type of poison used is not described. Why would these bone points be used along with the larger, sharper points of obsidian? Certainly the bones in Fig. 66, shown along with the claw bones and teeth of bear, could be effective for any type of animal. Although points might seem to hark back to the fossil, beveled, javelin-points described by Cressman, who studied the Lower Klamath Modoc, they are not the same nor do they resemble the bone cylinder points of the Cradle Culture at Clear Lake.

The butchering of large animals such as elk, bison and bear required good tools. In order to transport the carcasses from the kill-site to the village, the Modocs had to cut the animal into pieces small enough to carry by hand; they did not have the horse or travois. There were, of course, periods when the canoe could be used for transport. At other times, the dry lakebed provided a grassy plain over which to travel. In any case, the knives had to be carried to the kill-site by the hunters.

It must have been an exciting experience for the women, children and old men of Nightfire to watch for the return of the hunting party. With majestic Mt. Shasta in the background, the hunters would appear, accompanied by barking dogs and with whoops of joy. Some of the party would be carrying shanks of meat, others, the heads and hides of game. The hide of a bear would perhaps mean a full stomach of roast bear meat and a warm blanket. It might also mean the wailing chant of the death song and the light of the funeral pyre in the night sky of the island. Approaching a ferocious grizzly bear with a spear or atlatl doubtless called for both skill and courage. Both widows and orphans undoubtedly resulted from such encounters.

Two types of knives were used for skinning and dressing animals. Shorter blades were obviously mounted on a handle, Fig. 67. Those shown in Fig. 68 may have had a hide-wrapped handle on one end or have been carried as a simple blade.

Coyote and Dog

At the beginning of the historic period, Modoc Indians would eat neither dog nor coyote, considering them taboo. Such a restriction was evidently also observed in the old Cradle Culture at Clear Lake. There in the wind-blown sands of the ancient camps, the author found the bones of several dog skeletons. Each bone was in the exact position it had been left centuries before. Some of these bones were sent for study by university scientists. It was determined that at least three types of dogs were owned by the Cradle Culture people during the centuries they occupied the area. It is obvious that, had the dogs been a popular food, the bones would have been scattered.

Johnson reported the dogs of Nightfire to be short and squatty in shape. They were evidently good to eat as their numbers indicate dogs and coyotes equaled or exceeded the numbers of deer and antelope consumed. Fig. 69 shows dog or coyote jaws. Pictured with them are notched projectile points. These were by far the most numerous of any type from the early period of the second phase (about 6,000 years ago) until the fourth phase. The

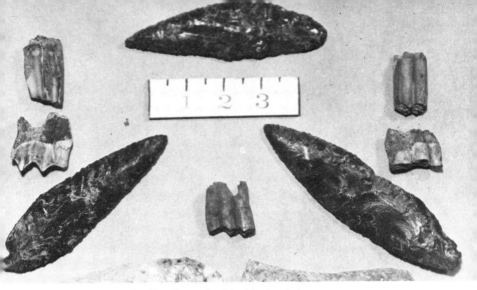

Fig. 68. Elk teeth with skinning knives.

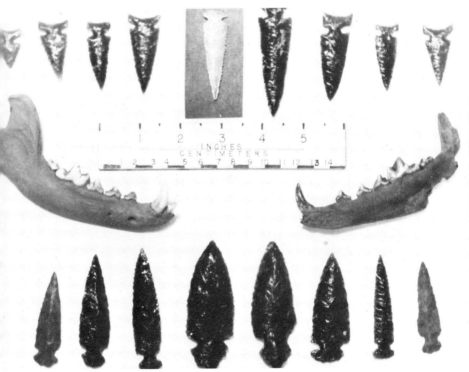

Fig. 69. Coyote or dog jaws with two types of early-phase points.

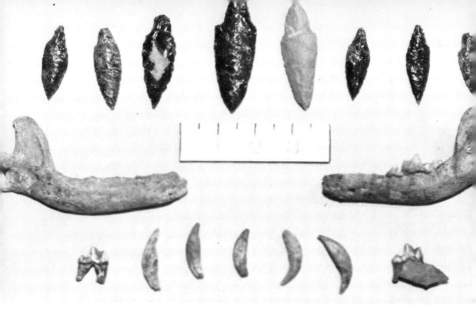

Fig. 70. Wolf jaws and teeth were not uncommon during the first 4500 years of occupation.

Fig. 71. Ancient sheep horncore trophy. (National Park Service)

two types of side-notched points made up about 59 percent of those found. Their popularity ended when the Gunther points appeared.

The diet restriction on dogs played no part in the life of the Nightfire Islanders. Grayson's study showed that dogs became a popular food during the beginning of the third phase, about 4,000 years ago, and remained popular for 3,200 years.

The wolf was consumed from the time of the founding of Nightfire. Fig. 70 shows an early-type projectile point together with wolf jaws. The particular shaped point shown in the figure made up only 2 percent of the points found at Nightfire. Oddly enough, the remains of the wolf disappeared at the same time period that the buffalo bones vanished.

Big Horn Sheep

The Big Horn Sheep is normally considered rather scarce, if not a rare animal. The rimrock country north and east of Mt. Shasta must have been an ideal range for them as the bone count in Nightfire indicated that they were as numerous as deer or antelope. They grew to a great size as shown in Fig. 71. Paul Haertel, Superintendent of Lava Beds National Monument, holds a sheep horn ranked second in size in the Boone and Crockett *Book of Records*. The dark-colored horn core held next to the head was found in the midden of Nightfire Island. It is nearly as large as the record set. A number of sheep skulls have been discovered in a large cave at the Lava Beds, that is now called Skull Cave. It is thought by some to have been a butchering site for the Modocs.

The sheep herds survived well into the historic period, long after the Modocs had abandoned their island village. The last native sheep disappeared, however, about the year 1910 A.D. Fortunately, the National Park Service has restored this fine animal to the region, Fig. 72. The sheep seem able to ward off the numerous local coyotes as the flock is increasing. Their habitat borders a road in the Monument where big rams, ewes and sometimes lambs can be observed on the side of a high rimrock mountain.

Fig. 72. Rams band together during most of the year.
(National Park Service)

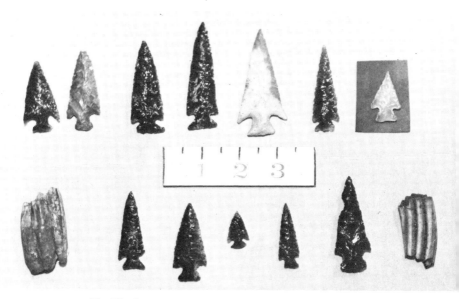

Fig. 73. Corner-notch points were popular when Nightfire
was first established.

The sheep teeth in Fig. 73 are shown with a group of corner-notched projectile points. Some of these points were found in the lowest levels of occupation in the white muck of the old lakebed, indicating that the style was brought with the Indians when the village was founded. They were as numerous as the side-notched points which disappeared when the Gunther points replaced them. In the first three phases of occupation, 7,000-2,000 B.P., corner-notched points made up 16.5 percent of the total.

Fire Treatment of Stone

The beautiful three-inch white point near the center of Fig. 73 is an example of the skill and stone artistry of the founders of Nightfire. A conscious effort to find colorful chipping material is evident throughout the occupation. Agate, chert, quartz and jasper provided a medium to display artistic talent. Flakes of a chert-like white material showed up frequently in the early phase but no source of supply could be found. Finally, three large chunks of the white stone were discovered together in a bed of charcoal. All had been burned and had turned white except a small corner of one stone. This clue gave away the secret of its source. The rock is called yadenite and was obtained at the site of a fossil geyser near the campus of Oregon Institute of Technology in Klamath Falls. The primitive craftsmen had learned that by burning the purplish stone, the color was changed to white and undoubtedly became easier to flake. A long trip by canoe was required to obtain the yadenite.

The blades and spears pictured in Fig. 74 were also from early-period paint and ash deposits. Such points were probably more prized for their beauty than for their value as weaponry. Studies of the styles of weaponry indicated the Modocs were very slow in making changes over the centuries; however, it can be seen that the large points in Fig. 75 are different from those in the previous figure. These are from the phase-four level and were used during the time when Gunther points were the most popular projectile point. Since the bow was most likely available, those pictured were probably mounted on a hand-held spear.

Antelope

Pronghorned antelope have shown a remarkable ability to survive. They were on the menu at Nightfire over 7,000 years ago when the island was founded and the numbers eaten increased into phase four. Thanks to the nearby wildlife refuge, these graceful speedsters can still be seen on the rock flats of Siskiyou County.

The polished bone knife in the center of Fig. 76 is made from the scapula or shoulderblade of an antelope. Edges of the bone still show how the user kept it sharp by grinding it with a scoria abrasive stone. The bone projectile points in the figure are all from soil levels laid down before the bow and arrow became available. To make them, a mammal bone was grooved lengthwise to the proper width for the point. The bone was next broken along the established grooves. It then became an easy task to grind it to the desired shape with a piece of volcanic scoria or other abrasive stone. Such points would normally be considered as the parts of fishing spears or other fishing implements. The presence of these—usually broken, in the cooking ovens—mixed with the bones of antelope, coyote, dog and deer, leads to the belief that these points were used principally as dart points for game hunting.

Elkhorn Tools

From the numbers of elk antlers and elk antler tools, it would be easy to conclude that these animals provided the principal mammalian-type food. Actually, Dr. Grayson's analysis showed that the numbers of such animals consumed remained about constant from the first phase to the last. The size of the bones and state of preservation no doubt makes them more noticeable than the bones of smaller mammals.

The massive horns of elk were not cut with large knives. Surprisingly, a simple obsidian tool—pointed but otherwise often poorly shaped—called a graver was used to pick away at the hard antler material, Fig. 77. When the horn was sufficiently weakened around the section where it was to be removed, a sharp blow

Fig. 74. The percussion-flaked points in the upper part of the figure do not fit in with the others. They are thought to be much older—probably found by the owners.

Fig. 75. Late-period spears were different.

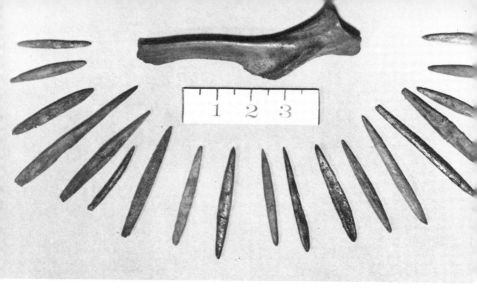

Fig. 76. Shoulder-blade knive with mammal bone points.

Fig. 77. A small graver could cut a large elk antler.

could break the remaining softer, more porous part of the antler. Further cuts with the graver readied the antler for finishing with an abrasive, rasping rock such as those in Fig. 78. Pendants, beautifully decorated armbands and tools such as harpoons were made from the antlers of elk. It seems almost impossible that the massive horns of the elk could be made into thin sections, then bent to the desired shape.

To prepare the antler material, Indians would first dig a hole and place rocks in the bottom. A fire would be laid on the rocks and allowed to burn until the rocks were heated to a high temperature. Green grass was laid on the hot rocks, and the antler materials, or sometimes wooden objects, were placed in the hole. More grass—sufficient to generate steam from the heated rocks—was placed on top, then the hole was filled with dirt and allowed to steam overnight. Such a steam treatment made possible the bending and shaping of the antler or wooden object. No doubt it was made easier to cut with the gravers. The simple abrasive rocks would rank rather low on the value list of collectors, but to the Modocs, whose survival depended upon the manufacture of tools and weapons, they would have seemed indispensable.

Mule Deer

Of all the animals hunted by the Modocs, the mule deer is one of the few that can still be taken by present-day hunters. These adaptable animals can be found in the tule marshes of the bird refuge and in the barren juniper habitat. They thrive on the manzanita-covered mountains of Siskiyou County and Klamath County, where the pine trees have been harvested or burned off. Mule deer, of course, provided food, but it is hard to assess the great value that the hides of these and other animals had for the Indians. Since tanning processes were known, both clothing and rawhide armor were made from skins.

The popular concept of an Indian is an individual dressed in fringed, beaded buckskin. Modocs and Klamaths did adopt buckskin dress but the fashion came, in or near, the historic period.

The Klamath deerskin robe shown in Fig. 79 is now in the Smithsonian Institution. It represents the more primitive garment used along with the feather blanket.

The sinew, bones and antlers of mule deer added yet another dimension to the Modoc economy. The deer antler in Fig. 80 shows how it was severed on the end toward the head of the animal by a graver. The obsidian tools in the photograph are from the lower, early levels of Nightfire. They have been flaked or knapped only on one side, leaving the other side flat. Called unifaced, they were likely used for cutting and scraping. Most of these show no evidence of having been fitted for a shaft or handle.

The projectile points in the lower part of Fig. 81 are surprising in that they are small enough to be used with the bow and arrow, yet they have great age. They were found sparingly by university excavators, and went out of use at Nightfire about 3,000 years ago. They made up about 9 percent of those found by the author. The triangular and U-backed points of all sizes were very popular with the Indians who inhabited Surprise Valley in California and Lake County in Oregon, during the period prior to the introduction of the bow and arrow. The points in the upper part of Fig. 81 resemble Gunther points but they are larger, more massive and much older. This type made up about 5 percent of those found in the first three phases of occupation.

Small Mammals

The otter jaws in Fig. 82 give evidence that the introduction of the bow brought bad news to the small mammals of Nightfire. The numbers of otter, beaver and rabbits going into the cooking baskets of the Modocs showed an increase when the bow and arrow replaced the dart point. The small, sharp Gunther-type points in Fig. 82 became the overwhelming favorite during the fourth phase of occupation. The single Shoshonean-type, side-notched point directly under number 3 in the picture is a clue to the very brief occupation of the previously long-abandoned village site. This type point was in popular use after the year 1,400 A.D. University researchers revealed finding no such points. The

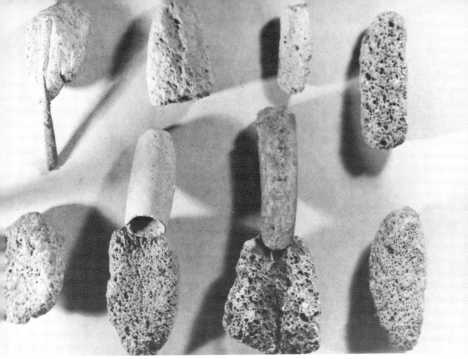

Fig. 78. Files and sandpaper of the stone age, made of abrasive rocks.

Fig. 79. Klamath deerskin robe. (Smithsonian Institution permit no. 77-11-310)

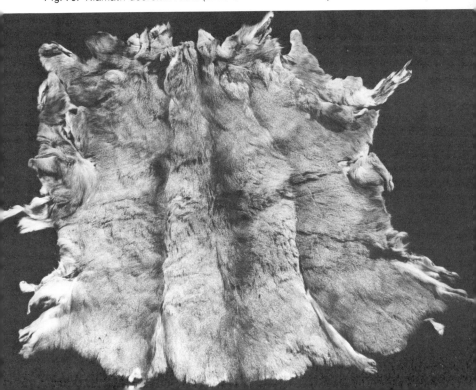

Fig. 80. Obsidian tools of the uniface variety, flat on one side.

Fig. 81. Small early points used before the bow and arrow.

Shoshonean-type arrow became popular with both Klamaths and Modocs after it was introduced. These arrows have been called Chiloquin points by the Klamath.

The jackrabbit was a major food source for the Paiutes, who occupied the Great Basin from Southern California clear into Idaho. The rabbits were captured by stretching long, fiber-woven nets on poles, then driving the rabbits into the nets where they could be clubbed. Paiute rabbit-skin blankets were common throughout the area the animal occupied. The rabbit was never quite as important in the economy of the Modocs. First, the competition from the numerous eagles and hawks held down the rodent population. Second, there is no evidence, either in caves formerly occupied by Modocs or in the rabbit bone count of Nightfire, that rabbit nets were used. The introduction of the bow and Gunther point explains the increase in rabbit consumption during phase four of occupation.

Marmots, sometimes called "rock chucks" were popular for food and are often mentioned in the legends of the Modoc. It seems likely that a snare would be the best method of catching them and their smaller cousins the ground squirrels, but the increase in small arrowpoints would show that they were also shot. In the late fourth phase, about 2,000 B.P. to 1,500 B.P., Gunther points—along with uncountable wooden points—were the dominant types used.

In the earlier phases there was a much greater variation in both the style and size of projectile points. The accompanying chart, Fig. 83, gives the numbers, types and percentages of points used in the first three phases at Nightfire. It is an adaptation of the one made by Dr. Garth Sampson but does not extend into the fourth phase. Analysis for the chart was done by Juanna and Terry Schafer. If the chart were to include the last two phases it would look very different.

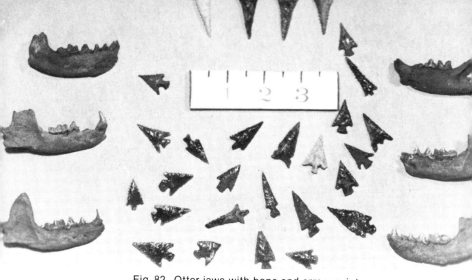

Fig. 82. Otter jaws with bone and arrow points.

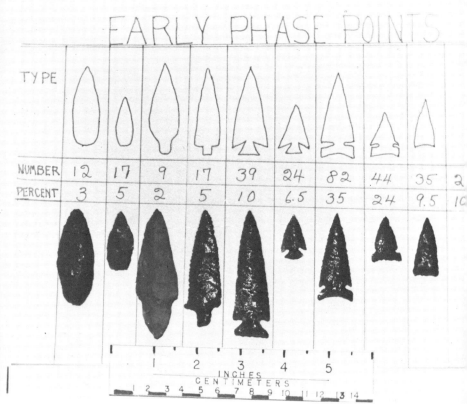

EARLY PHASE POINTS

TYPE										
NUMBER	12	17	9	17	39	24	82	44	35	2
PERCENT	3	5	2	5	10	6.5	35	24	9.5	10

Fig. 83. Early phase points.

5. NURTURE AND PROTECTION FROM THE MARSH

Vegetable Foods

Agriculture in the new world was first developed in Mexico. Scientists at the National Museum said that Indians of Mexico developed agriculture simply in order to survive. The animals upon which they were dependent were being killed off so fast that another source of food had to be found. Eventually the knowledge of food-plant growing spread to the southwest United States and to some eastern tribes. The Hohokam of Arizona were among those who brought farming techniques from Mexico, but these farming people became dependent on corn and lacked the protein provided by animal foods.

The Modocs found themselves at the opposite end of the nutritional scale. Their habitat provided an abundant supply of animal protein but the starches, so plentiful to the corn-growers, were in short supply. The growing of food plants was not practiced by the Modocs, who gathered native plants for harvest in their proper season.

Natural plant distribution is dependent upon climate, so gaining a knowledge of the climatic conditions was a part of the Nightfire research by the scientific team. The analysis of pollen samples is a valuable method of looking back over the centuries at former growing conditions. As fragile as it seems, pollen will survive the ages if it is laid down in sediment such as sandstone or in lake sediments like those at Nightfire. Pollen grains more than a million years old can still retain their shape and identity if they are properly extracted from the rock or soil in which they were deposited. Since the prevailing climate at a given period is directly related to the plant life, the soil strata will tell the investigator —called a palynologist—about the weather.

In Fig. 84, Johnson is boring in carefully prepared levels to gather pollen. Seventeen soil samples were taken, ranging in depth from the sterile clay-like soil at the bottom 1.7 meters deep, to the surface. Soil containing the grains of pollen was brought to the laboratory, where a difficult process of extraction and identification began. The soil was first boiled in chemicals, then treated with other chemicals to dissolve the silica (mineral content). The material was next placed in a solution with a high specific gravity (1.7) in order to float out the lighter material containing pollen grains. This, in turn, was placed in a centrifuge and whirled at a rapid rate to further refine the substance. This concentrated material was then placed upon a slide for microscopic examination in which the grains of pollen and spores were identified according to the plant from which they came.

Pollen studies indicate that climatic changes following the eruption of Mt. Mazama were not as pronounced as might be expected. There were traceable changes, however, which affected the lives and habits of the inhabitants of Nightfire. There were times when the waters of the lake rose so high that the original settlers had to leave their camp—including their precious stone artifacts. At one period the lake became deep enough that the tiny diatoms from the waters filtered down like fine snow to the bottom, covering some tools completely and leaving others partially embedded in the white mixture at the bottom. The crude, eight-inch-long blade in Fig. 85 was found embedded more than eight inches in the lake-muck bottom. By using obsidian hydration techniques, Dr. Larry Kittleman has dated the tool at about 6,500 B.P. The drawing is by courtesy of Dr. Garth Sampson.

Fig. 84. Pollen samples are carefully gathered and the depth measured by Dr. Johnson.

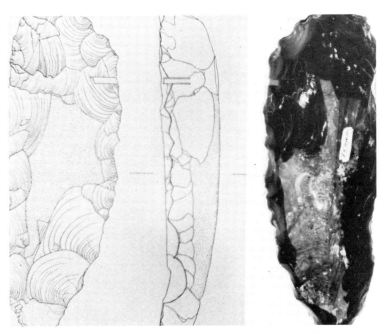

Fig. 85. The crude uniface blade was found to be more than 6500 years old.

Water Levels of Nightfire

When water forced the people from the site, waterfowl returned. Perhaps for several centuries, as they swam and walked about over the site, their droppings accumulated. This left a yellow layer of sand containing a sulfurous compound to indicate that the island was water covered for a considerable time. When the ducks returned, the hunters also returned, but not to live there, just to hunt. Intermingled with the yellow, wave-washed sand they lost many of the football-shaped bolas stones—probably a record of the birds that got away.

It seems impossible to tell how many times the water surrounding Nightfire rose and fell. It is also difficult to tell the causes of the water fluctuations. The period of time, 8,000 to 4,000 Before the Present, has been named Hypsithermal. Some scholars say the period was marked by increased rainfall; others say moisture decreased. Most agree that it was warmer during that time than it is now. The puzzling reasons for the changes in the lake levels are further complicated by the possibility that the rock fault at Keno, which controlled water levels in Klamath River, could have changed, as it apparently did at the time of the Mazama eruption.

During one period of high water, the growth of tules and marsh plants built a layer of peat and vegetable residue on the northwest side of the mound. The layer of white ash there now serves to tell of the marsh fire which roared through the accumulated dry reeds to consume the peat-like soil as well as all surface life.

Each time the receding waters allowed the Modocs to return to the creek-side camp, they built it a little higher. The added elevation provided a refuge for a greater interval during succeeding flood times. A long period of human occupation occurred from about 6,000 to 4,000 B.P. The tons of rocks, along with animal bones and charcoal, have left testimony of the time of occupancy. The alkali mineral of the lakebed preserved much of the animal bone remains while the softer plant materials vanished with decay.

Plant Classification by the Modocs

In looking at the vigorous and rank growth of marsh plants at the Lower Klamath Bird Refuge, one would assume that they are quite durable, yet many of them have to make a delicate adjustment to their habitat. They are especially sensitive to the water level that surrounds them. Without doubt, as the depth of the water level at Nightfire fluctuated, changes in the types of plants available made changes necessary in the Indian diet.

In a world where life depended upon finding the kind of plants necessary for nourishment, the ability to identify and locate them was more than an exercise in botany. Indians living in regions where agriculture was not practiced became experts in their knowledge of where to find the plants and in the techniques of preparing them to make them edible. The seasons of the year and the weather were of great importance to the hunting and gathering Modocs. A listing of their botanical products was given in the Lutuami language to Albert Gatschet in 1888. It is possible to identify some of the plants from Indian descriptions such as: mai (tule), kas (ipo), and puks (camas). Others such as kapiunksam, taksish and tchipsam cannot be related to either a common name or a Latin botanical description. Much plant-lore, as well as the pronunciation of the language that described it, passed along with the last generation of Lutuami-speaking people. Some of the most useful and important plant products of the Nightfire Islanders follow.

Tule

Since each Indian village had its own major source of food, it is not possible to say that a certain plant, fish or fowl was of the first importance to the tribe. If the people of Nightfire were to vote on "the plant they could not get along without," the election would, without doubt, be won by the tule, *Scirpus Americanus*, called mai by the Modocs. The reasons for its importance are many. It gave protective cover in hiding from the enemy. They could live with security in the close-growing plants which sometimes reached a height of 10 feet. Tules also served as a blind or camouflage for hunters stalking birds. As a food plant, tules would rank rather far down the preference list, yet they were always there in great abundance. In the spring and into summer they could be pulled and the tender, white tips, Fig. 86, chewed to extract the juices. The fibrous residue was discarded.

By far the greatest value of the tule was for basketry material. Some baskets, such as the large conical burden baskets and some storage baskets, like the one shown in Fig. 87, were made of whole tules. Note that in the upper part of the container, open spaces have been left to allow circulation of air through the contents of the basket. The bottom has cleverly been made solid to keep anything from falling through.

The larger house mats were also woven from whole tules. In order to make twined baskets like the very old trinket baskets in the figure, it was necessary to split the tules with the fingernail or with a basketry awl. The women working the wet fiber could, by deftly rolling it against their leg, produce a double string with a loop upon one end like that shown in the front of the picture. Such strands formed the main basic material for the many textile objects on the Modoc shopping list. Among these were: gambling mats, cooking ware, leggings, bags, shoes, cradles, quivers and hats. Most women and a few men wore basketry hats into the historic period. Fig. 88 shows the style was followed by Kientipus's (Captain Jack's) two wives. The lady in the center has a cloth hat but the design follows the basketry type.

A special study of Modoc basketry was made by Margaret Copeland, as a master-degree project, at the University of Washington. She said that while the Modocs were influenced by other parts of California cultures, their basketry showed alliance with the plateau and Great Basin cultures. Copeland's conclusions from the basketry study add further strength to the belief in the great antiquity of the Modoc tribe. She relates their techniques to the ancient cave discoveries by Cressman: "It would appear very possible that this twining is a very old feature of culture which the Modoc, along with many other tribes, carried with them to their

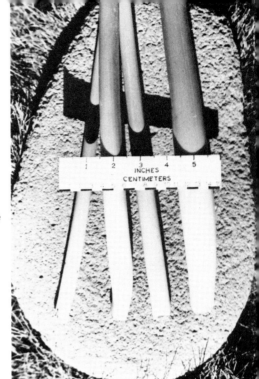

Fig. 86. The white portion of tule stems is tender and edible.

Fig. 87. Whole tules were used in storage baskets; split, twisted fiber in smaller baskets.

Fig. 88. Women's hat styles remained conservative, even after cloth was introduced.

Fig. 89. Maidenhair fern was used in Yurok hat, the dyed tule in Modoc.

present tribal location." The small amount of charred basketry found by the writer on a house floor of phase four supports this view and forms another tie to the ancient Cradle Culture.

There seems to have been no standardized list of names for basketry designs. More likely, each one used the name she visualized or thought about as she twined the basket. There were certain designs common to much of Northern California. Among them were: quail plume, flint, snake, step and arrow. Though the Modoc women used a wide variety of common designs, their basketry is easily distinguished from down-river baskets by the materials used and methods of twining.

In Fig. 89, two hats are shown: the one on the left, from a Northern California coastal tribe, uses maidenhair fern for the black pattern. The Modoc hat at the right uses dyed tules.

Lynn Anderson, a Klamath Indian, said, "Most baskets today are collector's items. The Klamath tule work is preferred by many because it is pliable. Unlike the stiffer basketry, the tule work will take an unusual amount of punishment. Also, the mats or baskets can be reshaped simply by soaking them in water and blocking to the desired shape."

The Nightfire way of life required the use of a boat or raft. It was a long distance to pine trees large enough for making a dugout canoe. It then took a long, difficult process for its manufacture. With the great abundance of tules at their doorstep, a balsa boat or raft could be made with much less effort. A skilled builder could probably make one in half a day. The balsa (tule) boat had widespread use in California. Doubtless, many darts and arrows were launched from a floating tule-reed duck blind. In historic times, a tule raft still served as a ferry over Link River at Eulalona, the present site of Klamath Falls.

The construction of boats, the weaving of mats, and the preparation of basketry materials all required the use of bone awls. The various shapes and sizes are illustrated in Fig. 90. Those at the top, the splinter type, were made by smashing a mammal bone, then sharpening the end on an abrasive stone. Those at the bottom of the picture have been carefully made and show much

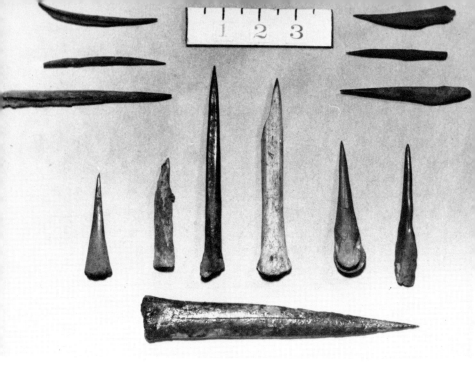

Fig. 90. Bone awls served diverse purposes.

Fig. 91. The summer house could be moved to the place where
the food was available.

use. The large one at the bottom would make a good dagger although it is doubtful that it was used as a weapon. Bone awls were found in the earliest levels, showing the great antiquity of basket making.

Cattails

The cattail (wiwi) was found to be abundant during the second and third phases. Growing in slightly shallower water than the tule, it served the same protective function for the Indians. Cattails mixed with tule fiber were used in basketry. It was important that they be gathered in the proper season, after which they could be soaked in water and then twined into baskets or mats.

The mats of cattail or tule served a major function in the lives of the Modoc. In the spring, as soon as the weather permitted, they would move out of the winter house into the more portable summer house. The summer house was made simply by bending willow poles and sticking the ends into the ground in the form of arches. When enough were placed for a support, a large mat was draped over the top and the summer house was ready for use, Fig. 91. The writer believes that some of the banded-stone weights were used to hold summer houses in place. The light, portable summer house allowed seasonal movement according to harvesting needs.

Cattail mats and loose cattails were used around the room of the winter house for beds. Gatschet's informants said that the buds of the cattail flower were good to eat. Art Chipman of Medford, Oregon, an authority on Indian foods, said that the roots of cattails were edible when sliced and fried. The main nutritional value was in the roots. These were dried for storage, then pounded and ground into a form which could be cooked into a kind of bread.

Camas

Bill Skeen, a Modoc Indian, was born near the spring that issues forth to form Sheepy Creek. When asked by the writer what was the principal plant food available during his childhood, it

Fig. 92. Camas bulbs resemble small onions.

Fig. 93. Ipos grow on scabrock flats where other plants cannot survive.

was expected that his answer would be either wocas or ipos. Surprisingly, his answer was "camas." Stone tools at Nightfire Island confirm Mr. Skeen's opinion. There were few evidences of the mano and metate, although we know that the Cradle Culture at Clear Lake contained numerous examples of these plant-processing tools.

The preparation of camas required neither rubbing nor grinding. The author was told by Mrs. Royce, who lived on the Klamath Marsh, the method of preparing camas. First, a pit was dug and then lined with rocks. A fire was next laid in the pit and allowed to burn out. Grass was now placed on the heated rocks and the camas bulbs were arranged on the grass lining the pit. More grass was placed on top of the camas bulbs, and rocks on top of the grass. Fire was built on top of the oven structure to heat the upper layer of rocks. After the rocks were thoroughly heated, dirt was thrown on top and allowed to remain overnight. Then the bulbs were removed. Mrs. Royce said that they were soft like figs and very delicious.

A great advantage of the camas was its keeping quality, according to Indians. It could be stored for more than a year. Hundreds of tons of small basalt and lava cooking-rocks were carried to the island, offering testimony to the many cooking ovens built there.

The camas plant still fills well-watered mountain meadows with blue spring flowers in the Klamath country. The camas bulbs in the territory of the Modoc were smaller than those pictured in Fig. 92. These onion-like bulbs are from the Calapooia country in the Willamette Valley. The name Calapooias is said to have been taken from the words meaning "camas burner." The camas plant throughout the Northwest has earned a special place in history. Treaties have been made over camas-producing lands and wars have been fought over their ownership.

Ipo

Ipo tubers are not true bulbs like the camas but more like small sweet potatoes. The flowering plants, which look like miniature parsnip tops, grow in great abundance in the scabrock flats of Modoc and Siskiyou counties, Fig. 93. Since the tubers occur at a depth of from four to six inches, a digging stick made of hardwood (mountain mahogany), topped by an antler handle, was used by the women in gathering the ipos, Fig. 94. The handle pictured differs from others used by the Modoc, as the hole for fitting the stick goes through the antler. It is more like the digging sticks used in the Columbia River region. Most Modoc antler handles fit on the top of the stick like a cap.

When used fresh, the thin brown skin on the ipo could be removed by shaking the ipos around vigorously in a basket. Many Modoc baskets had the ends of the reeds turned in to give a rough interior finish, Fig. 95. Whole ipos were dried and stored to be ground later into flour. Another method of preservation was to mash the fresh ipos into wafers or patties and dry them in the sun. In Modoc mythology, ipo digging seems to be mentioned more than any other gathering activity.

As an important food in most Modoc villages, the ipo would rank high, but at Nightfire the use was limited. University of Oregon excavators found only one antler digging-stick handle in the early fourth phase of the occupation. The one in Fig. 94 is fifth phase (recent). A few fragments of the bathtub grinding-slabs with turned-up edges were found but only rarely. This would lead one to believe that the grinding of ipo flour was quite limited. The distance of the island camp from the shore of the lake could account for the scarcity of ipo-processing tools.

Wocas

At one period, the bed of Lower Klamath Lake was a grassy plain supporting herds of buffalo and elk. Certainly, at other times it provided a habitat for wocas, the yellow water lily, Fig. 96. The blossom at left is about to lose its petals. The more mature bloom on the right shows the seed pod in formation. The dried seed pods could be stored but Indian women preferred to extract the seed for storage. Fig. 97 (left) shows the shiny seeds; at right,

Fig. 94. An unusual antler digging-stick handle. The hole goes through.

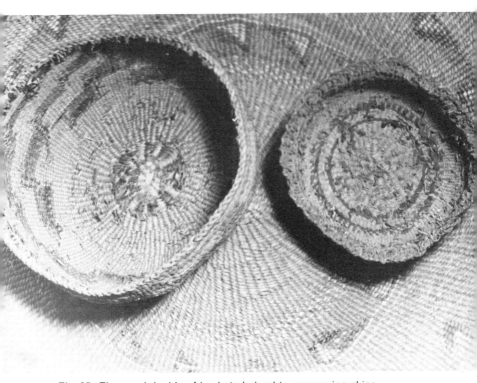

Fig. 95. The rough inside of baskets helped to remove ipo skins.

Fig. 96. Yellow water lily called wocas.

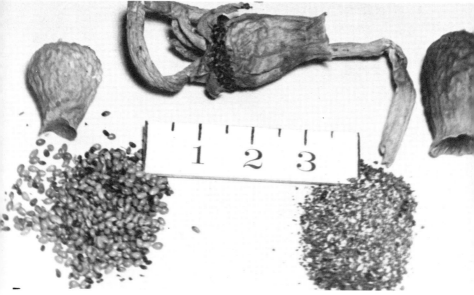

Fig. 97. Dried wocas seeds could be kept indefinitely.

the product after grinding on a lamch (metate) by Mrs. Nora Hawk.

All the equipment necessary for gathering this lily seed called wocas was available to Nightfire Islanders. Certainly the seventy centuries of occupation would have given them plenty of time, yet they did not develop the methods of processing wocas with the two-horned mano in the same way that their neighbors, the Klamaths, did. The fact that they spoke a slightly different dialect of the same language apparently had no effect upon the exchange of information on processing wocas. If wocas was eaten at Nightfire, perhaps a different processing technique than that used by the Klamaths was used, possibly pounding.

Few hand-grinding stones (manos) and even fewer large grinding-slabs (metates), were found by the author. Those found were in the very early period, second phase, and in the brief occupancy of the fifth period near historic times. The manos in Fig. 98 are all early but none show the signs of the rocking motion which was characteristic of the wocas grinder. In writing about the Indians, Cressman said that the two-horned mano was the result of a long period of development in the wocas-processing industry and occurred fairly late in the history of that tribe.

The mano shown in Fig. 99 was found in the light, porous lake muck under the island. At least 5,000 years old, it was used long before the invention of the two-horned mano, yet slight ridges can be detected on the top. Perhaps it is the primordial ancestor of those that became popular later. The small, dark mano at the right of the figure is one of the few evidences of the brief fifth phase of occupation. Perfectly flat on the grinding side, it was probably used on some type of small seed. The antler digging-stick handle (at the top of the figure) is more typical of those used by the Modoc, in that the hole does not go through the antler.

Arrow Leaf Root

By the year 1888, the arrow leaf root was known to the Indians by three different names: tchua (Klamath), wapato (Chinook), and potato (English). It occurs in a very restricted habitat. It must grow slightly under water with the bulbs growing very close together under three or four inches of mud. Those in Fig. 100 were found growing near Lost River. Very rich in starch, they are a little more coarse grained than a potato but resemble it in other ways. In the Willamette Valley they grew to a much greater length than those pictured. Indian women are said to have loosened the roots from the mud with their toes, causing the roots to float to the top of the water. The bulbs pictured were dug in January. Already the new shoot is forming to grow into the characteristic arrowhead-shaped leaf. After boiling and eating those pictured, the author would suggest a different method for connoisseurs of the tchua.

Onions, Wild Plums, Chokecherries

The Modoc word for onion was koipiluyeash. The wild variety in Fig. 101 likes to grow on the south side of rimrocks in sandy soil. They are noticeable for their beautiful purple bloom but have limited nutritional value; the small black seeds were ground to be used as flavoring. There was no archaeological evidence of the onion at Nightfire.

Wild plums grew in the rimrock country toward Mt. Shasta. Ripening in September, they were eaten by both deer and Indians. A little more sour than domestic plums, they are still prized when made into jam.

The seeds in Fig. 102 are those of the chokecherry. As indicated by the name, the flavor is sour and strong. When dried, they could be preserved to grind with the pounded meat of game animals or waterfowl.

Other Plant Foods

Nuts of the sugar pine were used for beads, as well as being eaten for food. It is unusual that those in the bottom of Fig. 103 escaped the ravages of time and weather. They were found on a house floor and were sufficiently charred to prevent decay. Pine-nut beads were perforated in a way to suggest their use was as sequins rather than beads. There has been no evidence that pinon

Fig. 98. Round quern stone at left with manos.

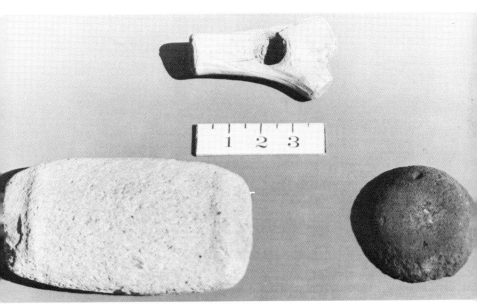

Fig. 99. Ancestor to the two-horned mano? Modoc digging-stick handle with late-period mano.

Fig. 100. Arrowleaf roots called Tchua.

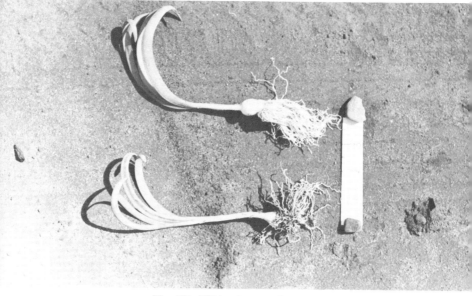

Fig. 101. Wild onions prefer sandy soil.

nuts, which were such a staple food in Nevada, were ever traded at Nightfire, although they were traded in later years.

The seeds of two types of fruit were also found on the house floor: the chokecherry necklace in the top, Fig. 103, and the pit of the native wild plum. Modoc women could find the wild plums in abundance around the hills and rims toward Mt. Shasta.

Other fruits known to have been used by natives were serviceberries, wild currants and elderberries, which played a minor part in the Indian diet. Huckleberries, a major fruit on the Klamath Indian food list, did not grow near the Nightfire village, but Indians were known to make long trips to gather these sweet berries. Charlie Ogle said that the people were so attracted to the berries that they would leave their crops unattended to go and compete with the numerous bears for the huckleberries.

One very puzzling question regarding Nightfire Island is why so many large stone pestles were found there, Fig. 104, in relation to the number of mortars. The university study showed almost three pestles to one mortar. The experience of the author leads to the belief that an even greater difference in ratio existed—perhaps five to one. One possible answer would, of course, be that the mortars were worn out and broken. It seems likely that in the preparation of foods, such as plums, berries or fruits, trays and mortars of wood were utilized. The women were known to have made preparations of dried fish or deer meat mixed with such berries in order to offer variety and to make the dried food more palatable. It is regrettable that the wooden implements have not survived the ages.

Only one quern stone was found at Nightfire. This, in the earliest phase, suggests that climatic changes took place or that use of the quern went out of style after such popular use in the Cradle Culture.

Mushrooms

There is no mention of fungus spores in the pollen count for 4-SK-4 but a rain in June brings out a wide variety of mushrooms from the decayed peat of the lakebed. The author has had the courage to eat three species of mushrooms and one of puffballs, Fig. 105. An expert in mycology no doubt could find other edible species. Puffballs will grow to a diameter of, twelve inches or more. The largest, *Agaricus crocodilinus,* shown in Fig. 106, grow abundantly. The person who seeks these finds that if they are not gathered soon after they appear above ground, they will contain a protein supplement in the form of small colorless maggots.

Like the wandering Paiutes of the Great Basin, Modocs utilized grass seeds, especially the tall rye grass that is nearly always found on their former village sites. However, they were never as dependent on grass seeds as the Paiutes, and the limited number of grinding slabs indicates that this seed was more likely pounded than processed on a milling stone. The straw of this tall grass was used as a material for making mats although it was too brittle for basketry. Indians were said to have saved the rye grass on their camps until other foods were exhausted so it would be available in times of need.

The plant foods in this chapter make up only a small part of those that were occasionally gathered and consumed by the Modocs. The main objective of eating was to stay alive until the next bird migration, fish run, or animal killed by a lucky hunting party. Survival was a commonly accepted goal which in some cases was not achieved. Gatschet stated: "They eat almost anything which is found in nature which is not positively obnoxious to health and which contains a particle of nutritive matter."

Nettle Fiber

The marsh culture of the Modoc was virtually held together by the fiber of the nettle plant. In addition to the uses mentioned in the section on fishing, the basket weavers often preferred to start the bottom of the basket with nettle fiber. It was softer, stronger and more pliable than other basket materials. The fiber is found in the bark around the outside of the nettle plant. Growing in unlimited quantities along the streams and marshes, it was gathered in the proper season. Then the fiber was separated from the

Fig. 102. These chokecherries grew on an old Indian campsite.

Fig. 103. Seed beads of chokecherry and pine nuts.

Fig. 104. Pestles were mostly double-ended and undecorated.

Fig. 105. Puffballs are never poisonous but soon deteriorate.

stem and twisted into surprisingly small strong threads to use for stringing beads, and larger cordage for snares and nets. The fiber, Fig. 107, (modern) resembles flax fiber used in linen and is almost as strong.

Sewing with the needles shown in Fig. 107 was evidently not the prevailing method of fabricating either skin or textiles as needles with "eyes" were found very rarely.

The use of the awl, especially the birdbone-splinter awls in Fig. 108, was much more prevalent through all phases of occupation. The stones in the upper center of the figure show that they were used to sharpen or polish the awls. The two double-pointed forks in the middle of the figure were made by simply rubbing a bird-bone on alternate sides against an abrasive stone until the double-pointed picklefork was finished. The single-pointed birdbone awls at the bottom were also common during all periods of occupation. Most, of course, were broken either by the user or from the pressures of time. They may have been used for sewing, basketry, or as "marrow-pickers" in eating.

Besides nettles, other non-food plants used by the Modocs were numerous. Sagebrush was one of these plants and, while the Modocs were not as dependent on the bark as were the Paiutes—who used it for cordage and sandals—it provided the main source of fuel. Even the earliest levels of occupation still contain fragments of sagebrush; some are actually mineralized.

Other Useful Plants

The Modoc, of course, used pine trees for canoes; juniper for bows; mountain mahogany for digging sticks and, as mentioned previously, arrow grass for arrowshafts. Many marsh plants have a narrow range of tolerance to the conditions under which they grow. Arrow grass (*Phragmites phragmites*) is a water-loving plant. It has been assumed by the author that a water habitat was necessary for its survival. Surprisingly, a clump of phragmites has survived near the old shore of Lower Klamath Lake despite the fact that water was shut off in that area when the railroad was built in 1910. The clump is stunted in growth since normally it reaches a height of six to eight feet, Fig. 109.

Fig. 106. Large mushrooms still grow at Nightfire.

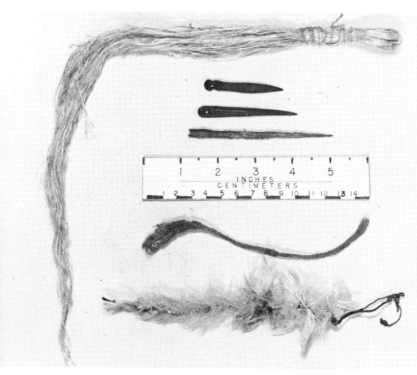
Fig. 107. Nettle fiber with bone needles.

Fig. 108. Splinter awls and awls of birdbone.

Fig. 109. This arrow grass is stunted but has survived.

Fig. 110. Coyote tobacco has a small trumpet-shaped flower.

Fig. 111. A surprising ancient angle pipe from the Fort Rock Desert.

There seem to be no fir or hemlock trees near the habitat at this time but, strangely enough, a decided increase in pollen from these two species showed in the soil samples representing the time period 6,600 B.P. and 4,600 B.P.

Did Modocs Grow Tobacco?

Indians of this region are not supposed to have practiced agriculture but there are two plants growing near the sites of the Modocs that strongly suggest they were transplanted or sown there purposely. One of these is the wild flag (iris), valuable for the strong fiber in making cordage. There is, of course, no proof that it was sown. The other plant which can be found on Sheepy Island, and near many other Modoc sites, is coyote tobacco or *Nicotiana attenuata*, Fig. 110. This plant has played an interesting and very complex part in the lives of the Nightfire Islanders.

A logical question would be, why did the Indians smoke? No one knows for sure but a partial answer may be found in a few sentences taken from a Modoc myth: the scene, in the woods; the five eagle brothers are hunting deer; they are approached by Yahyahaas, an evil spirit disguised as a one-legged man. "Can you feed me smoke?" asked Yahyahaas. "We have no tobacco," replied the eagle. "This earth will make people trouble if they don't carry a fire drill and tobacco. . .If people don't feed me smoke and make me glad, they must wrestle with me." People have been smoking to make themselves glad for a long time. Archaeologist Ben Wheat said, "Perhaps the earliest evidence of vice in America lies in the tubular stone pipe (or sucking tube) from the Jurgen's site." The date—about 9,000 B.P.—leads to the thought that smoking may have been a practice brought from Asia by the first Americans.

Another indication of the antiquity of the smoking habit is the stone angle pipe, Fig. 111, found in the Fort Rock Valley on a ridge where Indians had lived during a post-glacial period when the valley was a lake. Cattle had stepped on the bored pipe, revealing that it contained a stone filter. Notched on one side only, it differs from those on Nightfire, shown later. Stone angle pipes of even greater size have been found in the Clear Lake-Lost River Circle. Their age or relationship to the early Cradle Culture cannot be established.

After observing the smoking habits of Modocs and Klamaths, Albert Gatschet wrote: "Indians are not often seen to smoke continuously as we do. Those inhabiting the Klamath Reserve take a few whiffs from their small, often homemade pipe, then pass it to the neighbor and emit smoke through the nose. Sometimes they swallow the smoke for the purpose of intoxication. . .Cigars offered them are cut small and serve to fill up their tobacco pipe." The Modocs had a word for it: "titchewank" meaning, I like tobacco.

It was evident that titchewank was in full force at Nightfire Island. Dr. Sampson said that he had never seen an archaeological site where smoking seemed to have been so popular. There seems no doubt that smoking on occasion had a ceremonial purpose and at times was considered a social courtesy, but the amount of cake built up inside some pipes that were found would indicate frequent use by the owner.

Pipe Styles of Nightfire Island

The founders of the island brought more than one style of pipe with them; then, as ages passed, some new styles developed. One style, the plain tubular pipe, was always popular. The pipes in Fig. 112 answer the question as to whether the pipes were traded in from another source. The first early-phase pipe, in the center, is complete; the one at the left, partially complete; the other has been shaped only on the outside. All were made from volcanic cinder-like stone of local origin. The large hole in the completed pipe would indicate that a wooden stem was used in smoking it, probably from the pithy elderberry plant.

There were three methods of boring stone pipes. Most were first shaped on the outside, then drilled. Some were drilled with a "borer" like those pictured at the bottom of Fig. 113. Another method of drilling, certainly used on the long tubular pipes, was to place a few grains of sharp sand in the hole and then rotate a

Fig. 112. Old pipe in center and two unfinished blanks of scoria.

Fig. 113. Tools for scratching and boring pipes.

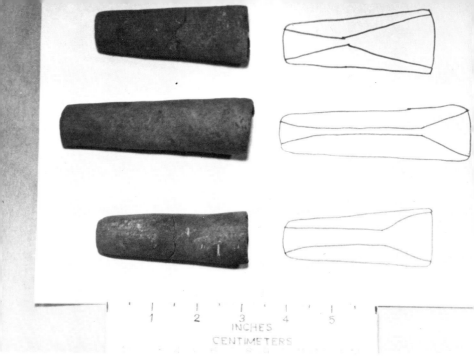

Fig. 114. Brown sandstone tubular pipes.

Fig. 115. Unusual bone pipe with two small stone pipes.

stick or reed in this hole, between the palms of the hands, in a manner to grind the sand into the stone of the pipe. As sand grains became rounded or dull, they could be replaced and the drilling continued. The long tubular pipes were drilled from each end. Sometimes the bore failed to meet perfectly.

Another method of making the hole in the pipe was to cut the stone with a sharp obsidian gouge or scratcher such as those in Fig. 113. In some cases, such as the one in the center of Fig. 114, the pipe has been first bored, then the hole has been enlarged by a gouge. All three pipes in the figure are from the early fourth phase and all are of red sandstone. The size of the bore would indicate they had been fitted with wooden stems.

Among Indians of much of Northern California, a very popular type of pipe was one made of wood. The end containing the burning material was lined with a small tube of stone or steatite. There have been no pipes found at Nightfire to indicate that such wooden pipes were made or traded there. An unusual bone pipe, Fig. 115, was found in an early phase-two level. In shape it resembles a large bead but an interior "cake" of burned material indicates that it had been smoked for a long time. The upper two pipes are later phase three and have been used with interior stems.

Although the tubular pipe was most popular, parts of several angle pipes were found. Those in Fig. 116 provide examples. The fragments are all from early levels. The ornamented pipe in Fig. 117 was found broken in a red paint deposit. It is identical with the drawing of another pipe from the site made by Southern Methodist University. Both the angles and the shape showed a relationship with Lost River Circle pipes from Clear Lake. The size is much smaller than some of the former, though, which have been found to reach a length of twenty inches or more.

All the archaeological research and writings indicate that the white sandstone pipe in upper Fig. 118 should not have been found. The Modocs were not supposed to have made a right-angle pipe until influenced by contact with Europeans. This one of sandstone was certainly not the result of white influence as it was discovered in the early second phase, about 5,000 B.P. The workmanship shows that it was first drilled, then the bowl was scratched out with an obsidian scratcher. The bore, that extends from the top of the bowl, was imperfectly done, resulting in a hole in the side. The smoker would need to hold a finger over this spot to make the pipe draw properly. The shape of the pipe may have been the result of an inventive maker, or more likely an effort to match the shape of a piece of sandstone previously carried from a distant place. The tubular pipe in the lower part of the figure is also of sandstone but it was made about 2,500 years later. Since the style does not resemble those used by tribes in the surrounding regions, it must be assumed that the white sandstone was traded in, then shaped and drilled by the resident who left it there.

Another feature of this pipe that is unique to the Lower Klamath Modoc is that it contains a small stone plug notched on each side for the passage of smoke. These I have called filters. They came in two styles at Nightfire: those notched on each side, and those which were bored in the center. Fig. 119 gives a closeup illustration of each type. The purpose of the stone plugs is thought to be for saving tobacco rath than for straining out the harmful tars and nicotine. Six pipes with filters were found on the village site. All those in Fig. 120 were filter pipes and all were from the fourth phase, about 1,500 B.P. The longest pipe found was 16½ inches in length and had been broken into seven pieces, probably when cast into a cremation fire.

Many more fragments of pipes were discovered than complete ones. Unfortunately, there seems to be no rule or method of determining the length of a pipe by measuring its diameter. Some of the long pipes have no greater diameter than the pink sandstone pipes shown in Fig. 121. These are all very old, early second phase. The one at the left is perfectly beveled on the stem end like an antler-hide hair dresser. Could it be that some wife was guilty of using a valuable tube to clean deer hides?

Fig. 116. Fragments of angle pipes.

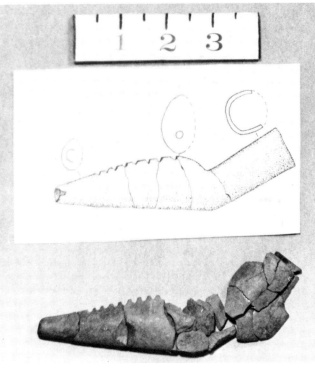

Fig. 117. Unusual angle pipe. (Southern Methodist University)

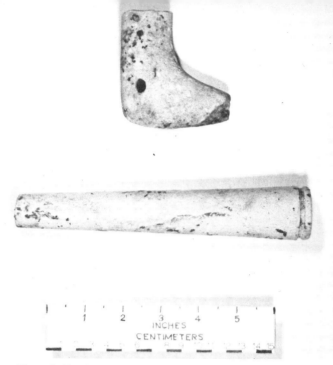

Fig. 118. Precious imported white sandstone was used for these pipes.

Fig. 119. Two types of tobacco filters, notched and bored.

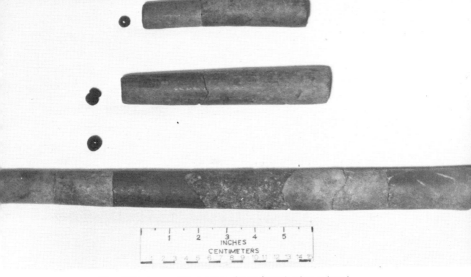

Fig. 120. Large filter pipes from fourth-phase level.

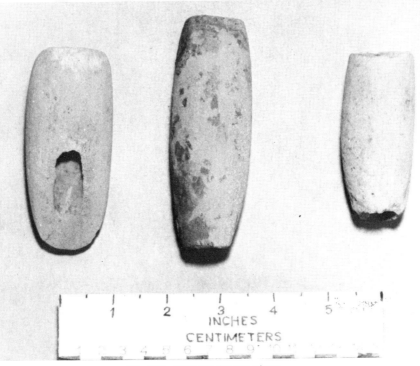

Fig. 121. Pink sandstone pipes.

There is no doubt that the Modocs had artistic talent. This shows especially in the basketry, but they never seemed to reproduce the human form either in their petroglyph pictographs or on their pipes. Nor did they make animal effigy pipes like the Mound Builders. The designs in Fig. 122 are geometric in nature. They show no fixed pattern—just the whim or dream of the maker. Another form of ornamentation used, Fig. 123, was achieved by grinding small indentations into the stone, in which disk beads were glued. In one similar piece of decoration, small holes were bored into a steatite pipe and then filled with red ochre. This pipe was found several miles from Nightfire and is not pictured.

Because the deposits of midden and refuse left by the people of Nightfire did not always occur in a completely level stratum, it is difficult to identify positively an age for a given artifact. It appears that the small round-bottomed pipes in Fig. 124 came into popularity after the angle pipes and large stone pipes of the second phase. Short, with a small bore and made of sandstone, they were likely used with a birdbone stem. University excavators found one with the stem in place.

Clay But No Pottery

When K'mu'kamtch, chief of the Indian gods, created the Modoc homeland and wrote the rule book, he must have said: "I will give you clay but you must not make it into pottery." The people of Nightfire were using clay 5,000 years ago. It would seem that a piece of clay, damp and pliable, was accidentally dropped on a mat, where it was imprinted with the pattern of the textile fibers. This clay was later fired, probably again by accident, thus preserving a mold of the textile and furnishing the clue to another aspect of Modoc life, Fig. 125.

It seems strange that, with the knowledge of clay molding, no pottery dishes were made by Modocs or Klamaths, especially when their neighbors, the Shastas, produced small pottery dishes and also small clay effigies of animal heads and fish. David Cole made the first discovery of pottery dishes in Oregon at Salt Cave, 12 miles from Nightfire. Had the Modocs decided to eat from

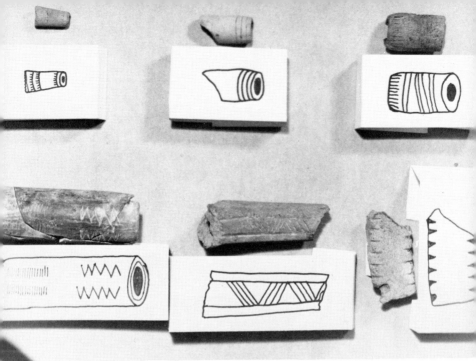

Fig. 122. Ornamented pipes were sometimes square rather than tubular.

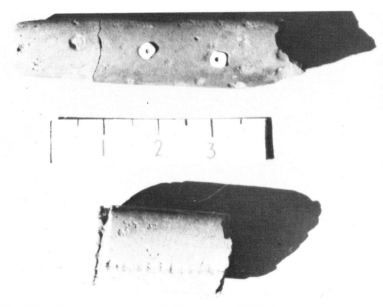

Fig. 123. Disk beads were mounted to ornament this pipe.

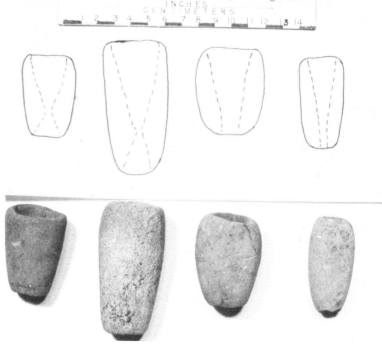

Fig. 124. Small pipes were used with birdbone stems.

Fig. 125. Basketry imprint left on gob of white clay.

pottery receptacles instead of only smoking from them, they would have preceded their cousins in Arizona in ceramic arts by several thousand years.

The brown clay pipe in Fig. 126 was undoubtedly made locally. It resembles the pipes of that time period, including the birdbone stem. The stem shown in the figure was not the original but was about the same size. The original disintegrated when exposed to the air. Another clay pipe used about 2,000 years later is shown in Fig. 127. Pale green in color, it still retains a birdbone in the stem end. This pipe has the largest diameter of any found at Nightfire—two inches. It is about five inches long, and the marks of the molder can still be seen imprinted in the clay. It has been broken into several pieces like most pipes found in the excavation. One piece evidently lay upon the island beach for a period, or was exposed to the waves by erosion, as it shows signs of weathering. Clay pipes are so unusual in Modoc country, it would seem that they were traded from another locality, but since coastal and neighboring tribes did not use this style of pipe, it must be assumed they were made by the users.

A study of the sources of the stones and clays used in pipe manufacture would provide an interesting story on primitive trade patterns. The source of one type of pipe material, steatite or soapstone, is well known. Deposits in the lower Klamath River canyon have furnished Indians of both California and Oregon with the shiny black stone which has been made into dishes, clubs and ornaments, as well as pipes. Soapstone pipes at Nightfire were the last type to become popular. Some were shaped with a tapered end so that they could be mounted with a birdbone stem on the exterior of the pipe, Fig. 128.

Fig. 129 shows steatite pipes apparently designed to be used without stems. Such pipes resemble those found on the Columbia River in Oregon and Washington. While the material is the same, there is enough difference in the shape to show that they were made by different people. In a few cases, pipes which were obviously designed to be used without stems have been later scraped off and mounted with an exterior stem. Perhaps the smoke became too hot, or some stone-age lung association convinced users that they should get away from *Nicotiana attenuata*, kinnikinnick, or whatever they inhaled "to become glad."

There were few marks of change in the way of life at Nightfire. Centuries went by with material culture much the same as in the previous thousand years. One development did take place, though, in the shaping of the pipes that gave the Modocs a cultural symbol different from that of surrounding tribes. It is the pipes with one, sometimes two, raised rings carved around them as in Fig. 130. One contrary individual decided to go in the opposite direction and carved a groove instead.

By the time Leslie Spier visited the Klamath Reservation in 1925-1926, where both Klamath and Modoc Indians were living, styles in pipes had undergone revolutionary changes. He remarked in *Klamath Ethnography*: "The pipe is commonly clay with a spherical bowl and a short wooden stem, but is sometimes of stone and discoidal. The more common stone bowl is elbow-shaped with the arms at an obtuse angle, made of sandstone, shaped and hollowed by pecking. . .The stem is elder with the pith pushed out. . .The manufacture of clay pipes by a non-pottery-making people is unusual; the only other use of clay is for making dolls."

Fig. 126. This brown clay pipe had a birdbone stem inside.

Fig. 127. Green clay pipe held bone stem.

Fig. 128. Exterior mounted stems on small steatite pipes.

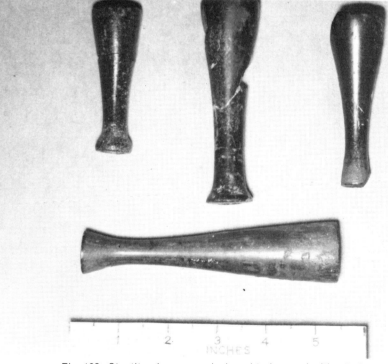

Fig. 129. Steatite pipes were designed to be used without stems.

Fig. 130. Modocs made rings on their pipes.

Fig. 131. Salmon bones in pleistocene sandstone.

6. THE FISHING INDUSTRY

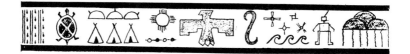

Fish Migrations

Nightfire Island was built with the east shore bordering Sheepy Creek. When the site was first visited, the appearance of the clear-flowing stream, with its proximity to the present lake, gave the impression that it was a fishing village. Excavation and research have, of course, proved otherwise; yet, there were times when catching and preparing fish occupied all residents of the island. There were probably also times when the empty bellies of the villagers depended upon the arrival of the fish for survival.

Some Indian groups were said to have given credit to the sage-hen for calling the fish up the streams. More likely, the local and friendly kuiks, or medicineman, claimed credit for the migration. A powerful man he must have been, for he was able to call sucker fish, like other kuiks but, in addition, he could call salmon.

There is no doubt that salmon spawned in Sheepy Creek. They were still spawning there in the 20th century when the construction of the railroad across the straits that joined Lower Klamath Lake and the Klamath River severed the channel, cutting off the migration route. The miraculous thing was the force that caused the salmon to enter the dark, warm waters of the shallow lake, then to swim unerringly to the cool waters of Sheepy Creek, past Nightfire Island to the sandy springs of the spawning ground.

Fig. 132. Modocs did not use charm stones like their Shasta cousins.

Fig. 133. Handles have been broken from these lamps.

Fig. 134. Oil-soaked fragment of a lamp.

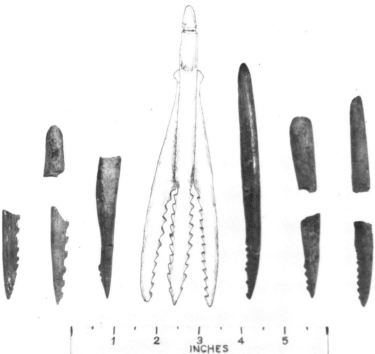

Fig. 135. Bone and antler points with Leister Spear drawing.

At first it was hard to imagine why the first pair of salmon would ever enter these waters. Then, a discovery of the pleistocene fossil-bearing sandstone layer near the Perry Langer ranch, Fig. 131, gave the answer. Here on a low ridge, a tan-colored, thin layer of sandstone is heavily laden with the bones of many kinds of salmon. Obviously the migration pattern was established during the time when post-glacial rains and streams coursed across the lakebed, cleansing it and providing a current strong enough to attract the first egg-laden fish.

John McKay saw the salmon run at Sheepy Creek. He said that they were dog salmon and not good to eat. Indications are that the Nightfire Modocs felt differently about the fish. They undoubtedly looked forward to the time "in the month of the third finger" when their kuiks would call the salmon past their island. The shamen along the lower reaches of the Klamath River were said to hang charm stones, such as those in Fig. 132, over the waters of the stream to keep the fish returning to the traps and nets of the fishermen. Norma Pollock, former curator of the Siskiyou Museum at Yreka, noted that a charm stone was found hanging in a branch over a stream, placed there to call the fish. There has been no evidence of a charm stone of this type in the excavation of Nightfire. Of course, there would be no way of telling if a "first fish" ceremony was celebrated in the manner of the Chinook on the Columbia River.

When the salmon arrived, even though scarred and discolored from the long trip through the Cascade Mountains, they must have been a welcome addition to the diet. The oil, too, could have been used in the stone lamps that the Modocs sometimes utilized to lighten the interior of their dark underground winter houses. Parts of four lamps have been found, Fig. 133, all in rather late phases of occupation, about 800 to 1,000 years B.P. They are made of a rather porous material to resist cracking, and show signs of fire. The depth of oil penetration into the stone can be observed, Fig. 134. Lamps and dishes of steatite, common to the California tribes on the west of the Cascades, were not found at this site.

The taking of salmon at Sheepy Creek should have been much easier than in the larger Klamath River. It would have been a simple matter to construct a weir to guide the salmon to one side of the creek, where they could be speared with a device similar to that pictured in Fig. 135. This is called a Leister spear. The head was detachable but connected by a cord to the shaft. The notched bone and antler points were found in the second phase, about 5,000 to 4,000 years B.P. Another type of spearpoint is shown in Fig. 136, from the same level. The fixed attachment is copied from a historic-period Modoc spear found on Lost River. It is now in the Favell Museum in Klamath Falls.

Tui Chub Traps

If the salmon run was spectacular and exciting, the taking of the tui chub was just the opposite. Yet the counts of the fishbones, especially in the last two phases, show that they were a more important element in the diet than salmon. Tui chub bones are easier to identify. Over the years, the author has found numerous sets of tooth-like fishbones and assumed that they were the teeth of a much larger fish. Dr. Richard Wilson, Fig. 137, caught some for the Nightfire study, removed some of the gill-rakers (pharyngeal bones) from the throat of the fish, and finally proved to a hard-headed unbeliever that they were not fish teeth.

Why were the tui chubs so popular in the Modoc diet? Certainly not because they were preferred to salmon and suckers but, like the lowly tule in the plant diet, they were always there and usually in abundance. These fish are chubs about eight to ten inches long when mature. They still swarm in large numbers in Sheepy Creek. Tui chubs also exist in great hordes and in most lakes of the Klamath country. In the 1960's, a bacterial disease infected them. The resultant millions of dead chubs floated ashore on Klamath Lake and caused odor problems, making some resorts on the lake virtually vacant. Oddly enough, the disease had little effect upon trout. No other such occurrence has been known in historic times.

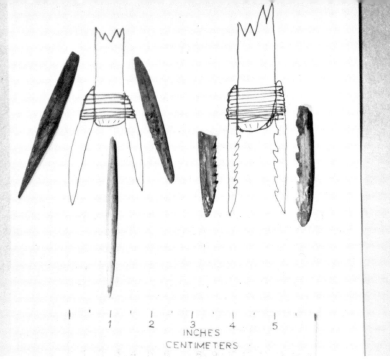

Fig. 136. Beveled bone and notched points.

Fig. 137. Dr. Wilson with tui chubs.

The easiest way to get tui chubs would be to dip them from the stream while standing on the shore or walking along the shore. But even if the chubs were numerous, net dipping would soon reduce the supply in the creek, and other methods would be necessary to catch the chubs. There is a clue in Modoc mythology as to how this was done: "Old Kulta was fishing. He called to the fish and said, 'I want to feed that young man.' Then he put his basket in the edge of the water and said, 'Come now—come into my basket.' Right away his basket was full of fish."

The basket used by Kulta in the legend, Fig. 138, was observed by A.B. Meacham, superintendent of the Klamath Indian Agency, about 1868: "The Klamath mode of taking fish is peculiar to the Indians of this lake country. A canoe-shaped basket is made, with covering of willow work at each end, leaving a space of four feet in the middle top of the basket. This basket is carried out into the tules that adjoin the lakes and sunk to a depth of two or three feet. The fishermen chew dried fish eggs and spit them in the water over the basket, until it is covered with eggs, and then retire a short distance, waiting until the white fish come in large numbers over the basket, when the fishermen cautiously approach and raise it suddenly until the upper edge is above the water, and thus entrap hundreds of fish that are about eight inches long [undoubtedly tui chubs]. These are transferred to the hands of the squaws and by them are strung on ropes or sticks, and then placed over fires until cured, without salt, after which they are stored for winter use. This fish is very oily and nutritious and makes a valuable food."

Since Shastas and Hat Creek (Atsugewi) Indians bordered the Modocs on the west and south, there can be little question that through trading and the skills of captured slaves, their style of fishtraps would have been available at Nightfire. The long, conical traps, Fig. 139, were used in what is now Lassen National Park. These were baited on the inside. Mrs. Selinda La Marr explained that a removable ring on the end enabled the fisherman to pour his catch from the trap.

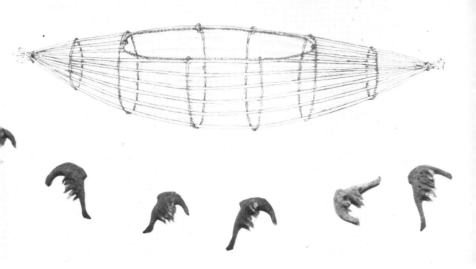

Fig. 138. Tui chub trap as described by Meacham. Gill rakers at the bottom.

Fig. 139. Hat Creek Indian trap used in Lassen Park for trout.

Taking Trout on the Sprague

The Sprague River Valley, east of the town of Sprague River and toward Gearhart Mountain, was occupied principally by the Yahooskin Snakes, a branch of the Paiute. These Indians told Alfred Collier of taking trout when the waters of the Sprague were low in the summertime.

A mat of woven willow was made about the width of a blanket and long enough to reach across a narrow riffle in the river. The willows were spaced wide enough to allow water to flow through without washing away the mat. The device was placed across the river with the downstream side on the bottom; the top extended above water on the upstream side and formed a ramp. After placement of the willow mat, members of the fishing party would go into the deeper water downstream from the ramp to create a disturbance. As the frightened fish dashed upstream, the momentum of their flight would carry them out of the water on the upper side of the willow ramp, where they could be picked off by fishermen waiting there.

Net Weights

Gill-rakers of the tui chubs are found on all sides of the eroded shores of Lower Klamath Lake. Certainly the Modoc, in order to compete with the pelican, had to have successful methods in taking the fish. Judging from the net weights found, the shallow waters of the lake did not lend themselves to the wide variety of nets common on Upper Klamath Lake. Weights on Lower Klamath were scarcer and more limited in variety. In the north part of Nightfire, a few roundish, banded-stones were found, Fig. 140. These could have been part of a set—perhaps on a seine lost and not recovered by the owners. The yellow stains of the "duck-muck" level can be seen on these weights, indicating that they can be dated in the second phase. Since fish and ducks were both taken with nets, there is no positive explanation for the use of the banded stones.

Other parts of the excavation yielded a few of these stones during the second and third phases but showed little relationship

Fig. 140. Banded stone weights for net or trap.

Fig. 141. Unusual weights possibly used with a drag net.

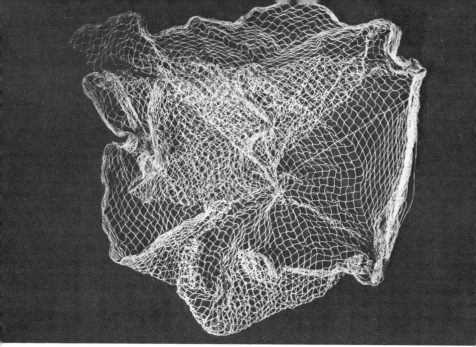

Fig. 142. Klamath net used for dragging behind canoe. (Smithsonian permit no. 77-11-310

Fig. 143. Deep-water canoe used with oars. (Favell Museum)

to the tui chub gill-rakers. It should be explained that while fish-bones appeared throughout the 7,000 years of occupation, the author suspects that most of them decayed unless they had been burned or were protected in ashes, etc.

The unusual stone weights pictured in Fig. 141 have never been professionally identified but they are thought by the author to be fish-trap weights, or for use on a drag net such as the one in Fig. 142. The completed one, with holes bored through, was found in the white muck of the first phase. The uncompleted one at right was in the third-phase level. Such stones have also been found at Clear Lake, Tule Lake and on Lost River.

Weights with a single perforation are common on the Columbia River and in nearly all fishing cultures. Those with two holes seem to be unique to the Modoc and Klamath.

Canoes and Boats

Attending the fish traps, as well as other food-gathering activities, required the use of a wooden canoe. Modocs made two types of canoes, each for a specialized purpose. The "vunsh" was a larger canoe which would carry four or five people. Propelled by wooden paddles, these canoes were useful on open water. They were safer in a wind-whipped basin where communication with the shores could be made only by boat.

Bill Skeen, a Modoc, born at the head of Sheepy Creek near Nightfire Island, told the author that he remembered seeing his grandfather's canoe on Laird's Bay. He said that it looked as big as a battleship to a small Indian boy. Fig. 143 shows a vunsh deepwater canoe at the Favell Museum in Klamath Falls.

The smaller canoe, called "vunshaga," would support only two but was much better for use among the lily pads and tules. A vunshaga was necessary in gathering wocas seeds, duck eggs and basketry materials in places the larger canoe could not be maneuvered. It was propelled by a pole, with the operator kneeling in the front of the canoe. The pole was split at the end and a stick or bone inserted to prevent it from sticking in the muddy bottom of the marsh. At the end of a gathering trip, the small canoes were often used as a receptacle or trough for processing the gathered foods, Fig. 144.

Either type of canoe must have been a valuable possession on Lower Klamath Lake. Pine, fir or cedar trees were used in making them. Getting the log to be shaped to the village was the first job. The nearest pine logs that could be floated in would have required a ten-mile trip to the Klamath River near Keno. Floating a log to Nightfire would have been much easier in the spring, for then the waters of the river were higher and would be running into the lake. In the fall, the trip through the straits would go against the current as the waters flowed out from the lake. To carry the logs overland might have been closer but would have required more effort. It seems impossible in the case of the large vunsh.

The outside of the Modoc canoe was usually left in the shape of the log from which it was made. Both ends were tapered the same, then the log was hollowed out until the shell was quite thin. It was so thin, in fact, that it was necessary to leave it in the water to prevent warping or splitting.

In the hollowing-out process, fire was used, then the charcoal was removed with gouges such as those in Fig. 145. Each gouge shows a very sharp edge as though hardened by a special process. None appears to have been pounded with a maul; however, a most unusual gouge of buffalo bone is shown in Figs. 146 and 147. This bone has been drilled out to a depth of about three inches so that a handle could be inserted in the end. This handy tool could also serve as a spade and would not be bad as a weapon. When other work on a canoe was finished, abrasive stones were used both inside and outside to smooth the entire boat. The author has not heard of painting or decorations being used on Modoc boats.

Wood-Working Tools

In addition to canoe building, tools found in the midden of Nightfire Island indicate that numerous other woodworking projects were carried out. The Modocs did not have axes but used

Fig. 144. Small dugouts with split pole.

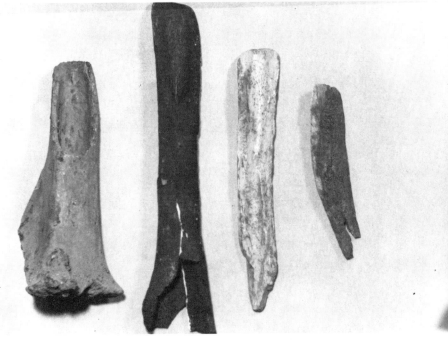

Fig. 145. Bone gouges were all quite sharp.

wedges made from the antlers of deer and elk. Those at right in Fig. 148 show that they had been bound by rawhide or sinew to prevent their flaking off when struck with a maul of wood or stone. The one at left shows flaking. Judging from the great number found, the antler wedges and mauls must have been employed for other wood-splitting jobs in addition to canoe building. House rafters, fish weirs and drying racks would be among other uses for the splitwood.

Mauls were also numerous through all the years of occupation; perhaps not so numerous, though, when it is considered that if only one were deposited in the soil each year, it would result in 6,000 of them. The styles of wedges did not change throughout the years but the style of mauls changed slightly. The mauls were, of course, used sometimes in food processing as well as for pounding. Mauls found in first and early second phases were smoother and generally bell-shaped at the bottom. Also, the handles were more rounded, as if they had been used as pestles, Fig. 149. Third-phase mauls found in the angular rocky layer of the midden had a more pronounced shoulder, while most handles did not indicate their being used as pestles, Fig. 150. Fourth-phase mauls were less artistically made. They seem more related to the canoe industry, less to food processing, Fig. 151.

Suckers

It is impossible to know the types of sucker runs that originally occurred in Sheepy Creek or to determine the time they occurred, but the sucker looms large in Modoc legends. Bone counts show that the lamps of Nightfire Island could have burned on winter nights with sucker oil. They are an oilier fish than the salmon. Four species of suckers are still making migrations in the Williamson River. Without doubt, some would have made similar migrations at Sheepy Creek until the waters of the lake were cut off from the Klamath River.

Members of the sucker family are common to many of the shallow lakes of the Great Basin in Northern California, Oregon and Nevada, Fig. 152. Fishermen still snag them with triple hooks

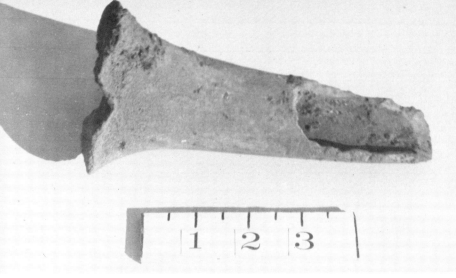

Fig. 146. Buffalo bone gouge.

Fig. 147. Hole drilled at the back provided a fitting for a handle.

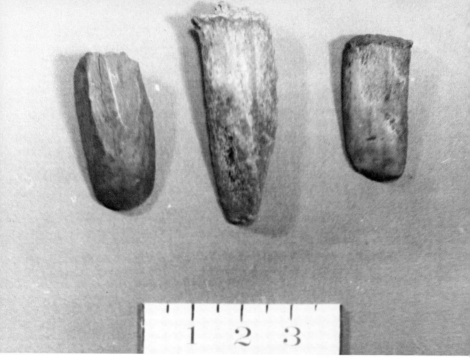

Fig. 148. Antler wedges show evidence of having been wrapped at the top.

Fig. 149. Early-period mauls.

and erroneously call these fish "mullet." Unlike salmon, they do not die after spawning but return to the lake. Indians well know the different species of suckers, as well as their habits. Glen Kircher of Chiloquin, who has learned many words in the Lutuami language, told the author the following Indian names for suckers: The yan runs in late March and weighs about 2 pounds. The koptu runs in April and weighs from 4 to 8 pounds. The big sucker, the tsuam, runs in May and weighs about 20 to 25 pounds. During their migration in great numbers, large suckers jump and cavort as though in play. In the Williamson River, they are accompanied by small suckers (hishtish) and lamphreys. The time period for the sucker migration is brief—only about three weeks.

To be properly utilized, the bountiful harvest of food required a method of preservation that would take care of large quantities. It also had to be accomplished without salt or other preservatives. The dry spring winds and high-altitude sunshine helped in the curing process. The fish were split and hung on willow racks as in Fig. 153. Sometimes slow fires were used to help keep flies away from the drying fish. A good job of drying could mean a longer period of storage which, in turn, meant less hunger during the winter.

Other Fishing Methods

Fig. 154 shows three types of points used in taking fish. The elkhorn barb and small obsidian point are from the fourth-phase levels. The large obsidian barb is from a much older second-phase level.

Fishing with a single line was never very popular with the Nightfire anglers. There are a number of reasons for this. A Paiute informant told Isabel Kelly of the University of California that the bone gorge was not suitable for small-creek fishing. Another problem is the shallow, dark waters of Lower Klamath Lake. Trolling a baited gorge behind a canoe could be unsuccessful because, even if game fish were present, they would be unable to see the lure at any distance. There is evidence, however, that some single-line fishing was done there. More than likely, the bone gorge or hook assembly was allowed to settle on or near the bottom in the same way the Haida Indians bait fish on the northwest coast.

The Lutuami word "ulawa," meaning "to watch for fish at an ice hole," offers a clue to another fishing method. Either the bone gorge could have been used through the ice, or watching could have meant "watching with a spear."

Most small bone objects found at Nightfire have been broken fragments. However, enough were intact to show them to be components of the line-fishing hooks in Fig. 155. Such hooks were in use at the beginning of the historic period. The more delicate bones under the gorge seem fragile for use in fishing. Since it was found with the single stone weight (lower right), it has been photographed with the fishing gear. It may have been a nose ornament.

Most methods of fishing require good cordage lines, nets, sieves or traps. They need skilled workmen and a fiber that will hold together in the water over long periods. Fortunately for the Modocs, an inexhaustible supply of such fiber was available nearby in the bark of the common nettle plant. The fiber can be spun into heavy cordage but the strength is such that fine string-like thread has been utilized. The charred remains of one such string have been preserved and can be seen wrapped around a birdbone by its maker, Fig. 155 at lower left. The valuable nettle fiber was used for many purposes, including string for beads and for hairnets.

The large migrating fish were important to the livelihood of the Nightfire Islanders but two other small species that lived in Sheepy Creek and the nearby lake the year around were utilized also. Since the swift-flowing stream never froze over, the importance of these lesser species should not be underestimated.

Peter Skene Ogden, the first man to leave a written record of the Klamath country, passed through with a trapping brigade in the winter of 1826. He wrote in his Journal: "We succeeded in trading at a cheap rate 40 dogs and some small fish not more than

Fig. 150. Middle-period mauls.

Fig. 151. Late-period phase-four mauls show a difference.

Fig. 152. Middle-size sucker, koptu, about 24 inches long, with burden basket.

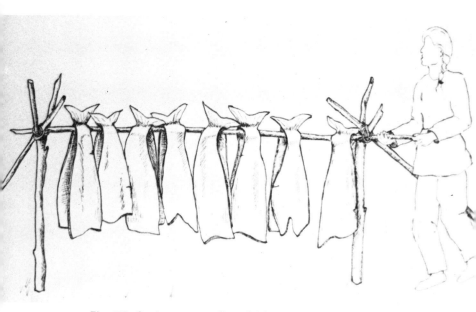

Fig. 153. Suckers were split and dried—usually without smoke.

two inches long." It is doubtful that they would be mentioned here as an Indian food were it not for that Journal entry. An inquiry sent to the fish expert, Dr. Dick Wilson, brought the reply that the fish were dace, a tiny fish about three inches long. Dace still thrive in the clear waters of Sheepy Creek, where motionless blue herons wait for one to come close. A willow trap would be too coarse to hold them. A sieve would allow the quick-darting minnows to escape. A small, hungry boy perched on the creek bank with a dip net could probably capture enough for a meal.

Turtles and Mussels

Turtles have survived millions of years while many of their relatives have been extinct. They seem likely to continue to survive for they are still abundant in the watercourses of the Klamath country. Modocs ate roasted or boiled turtle for almost 7,000 years and did not seem to reduce the numbers of the reptiles on Sheepy Creek. Although they were eaten in all phases of occupation, their shells were not used for rattles as in some Indian cultures. Only one specimen could be considered a turtle-shell ornament.

Fresh-water mussels were enjoyed for their flavor rather than for their beauty. They have been said to be one food that the Indians could gather in winter. The species native to the Klamath country is found on the soft bottom of streams and lakes, Fig. 156. Since they occurred in shallow water, they were easy to catch. These shells were not found in the first and second-phase deposits, possibly because of decay, but they were abundant in third and fourth-phase levels, especially in a caliche layer. The tightly packed, mineralized soil preserved them. Few shell ornaments have been found except those made of ocean shells.

Eels

It is doubtful that eels supplied many calories in the Indian diet but they seemed to have a special place in their mythology. Actually, the eels in the Klamath country are not eels but lampreys. They made spawning runs early in the year to deposit their eggs

Fig. 154. Fishing points with salmon vertebrae.

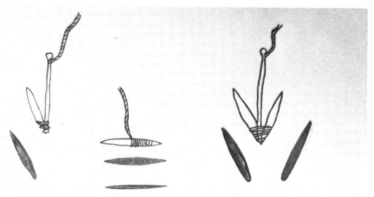

Fig. 155. Fishhook types.

Fig. 156. Fresh-water clams or mussels.

in sandy springs. In the process of the spirit quest, it was thought that by diving deep into the waters where the eels were spawning, great bravery was gained as well as strength and power.

A unique discovery was made by Oregon State University scientists during a study of the Williamson River mullet run. A new species of lamprey was found which was about eight to ten inches long. It spent most of its life in the lake, migrating in the spring of the year for the egg-laying cycle. When the Oregon State University Department of Fisheries called for a suggestion for a name for the new species, the word "kawe," the Indian word for eel, was suggested. If the name is adopted, it could be a little difficult to find a Latin pronunciation for a Klamath Indian word.

7. THE MODOC WAY OF LIFE

Winter Houses

Winter in the high plateau in the Klamath region was a time of trial for the ancient people who lived there. The altitude of over 4,000 feet created many problems. Migrating birds were gone and some animals in hibernation. Snow made land travel difficult, while ice prevented travel by canoe. Hardest of all was the penetrating cold—sometimes twenty degrees below zero—often made worse by the wind. The remarkable Modocs survived by inventions which made their adaptation to this severe climate possible. One invention was the feather blanket which they called "duck-skin" blankets. Another was the winter house or earth-lodge, which they referred to as a "mud house."

The houses varied in size from small ones of six or seven feet to others of over thirty feet in diameter. Cressman, who excavated several Klamath earth-lodges, said that the Indians did not always build them in the way they were supposed to. He told the author, however, that the structures described by Spier had certain features that could be considered typical. A circular pit was first constructed. Then four to six posts were erected near the center to support the cover and leave room for an entry through the roof by way of an inside ladder. The drawings in Figs. 157 and 158 are similar to the construction described by Spier. The four upright posts were connected by horizontal timbers.

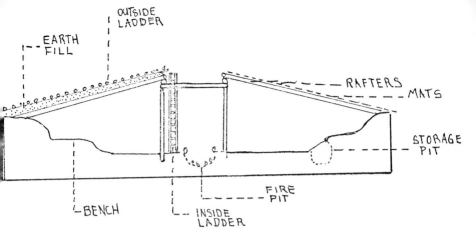

Fig. 157. Cross section of a winter lodge.

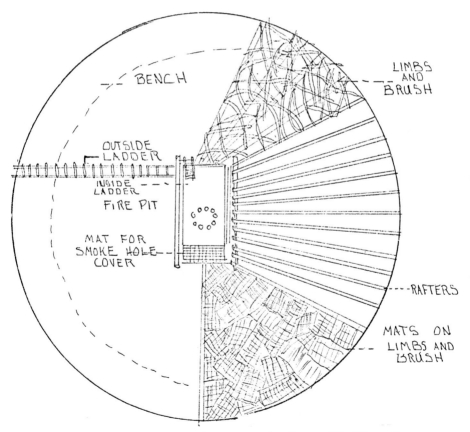

Fig. 158. Rafters, then branches, mats and earth completed the roof
of the winter house.

Rafters were then laid, sloping to the edge of the excavated circle. On the rafters were placed smaller limbs—sticks or bark when available—to provide support for the tule and cattail mats which were the next layers applied. Wren Frain, a Shasta, who once lived in the canyon of the Klamath River, said that, many times, loose tules and cattails were placed upon the rafters, possibly for insulation but more likely to keep the dirt from falling through.

After the mats had been applied, dirt was carried to cover all the roof except that part in the rectangle between the posts. This was left open as an entrance for the residents and an exit for the smoke. The firepit for cooking and warmth was directly below the smoke hole. Mats were placed so that the smoke hole could be closed when desired. The last feature of the house was an outside ladder leading up the slope to the entrance hole from the edge of the roof. Rungs of this outside ladder were laid in notches. The inside, more vertical ladder, had to be supported by the forks of limbs, or tied with cordage or rawhide.

Cressman found the floors of the excavated pits to be usually saucer-shaped rather than level. The elevated rim of the "saucer" sometimes contained a shelf for sleeping quarters. Tules, mats and skins served as padding for the beds. The underground part of the winter house contained pits or caches for the storage of dried foods and roots. Several Modoc legends relate thievery and mischief in these storage pits.

A slightly different version of the Modoc house was given by A.B. Meacham, one of the few men actually to inspect the inside of such a house. He reported: "The Modoc town was composed of thirteen lodges built after the model of Klamath Indian houses. A circular oblong excavation, twenty or thirty feet in length and twelve feet wide, is first made." His description differs from that given previously in a few respects. The winter house was oblong rather than round; the inside ladder was made of rawhide; the outside had no ladder—just steps in the earthen roof. The rocks for the firepit in the Modoc house retained the heat when the matting cover was pulled over the smoke hole. Meacham said: "The window, door, and chimney are one and the same."

It must have been a great effort to dig the necessary excavation for the winter lodge without shovels, hoes or buckets. Only stones, bones and baskets were available. The methods of digging at Nightfire are unknown but the soil preserved many of the implements of antler and bone.

During the early stages of occupation, while the island was being built, a great many tools and fragments made of basalt were used. Since the nearest mountain, called Sheepy Ridge, was made up of this gray, colorless rock, it was only natural that the Indians should use this rock, especially since it would require a tiresome and dangerous journey to obtain the nearest obsidian. Basalt, while often utilized, did not lend itself to artistically made tools. Most of the items found are simple flakes but purposely shaped, Fig. 159.

Two basalt tools shown illustrate greater skill and seem more specialized in their function than the flaked tools. One is the pick-shaped stone, the other is the triangular tool which resembles some of the hoes of the Hohokam of Arizona. The pick has been sharpened and may have been mounted by embedding it in a wooden handle. The triangular basalt has been carefully sharpened as though made for a saw or knife. The statue from Jalisco, Mexico, provides a picture of one of the ways stone or obsidian tools were strapped to a handle, Fig. 160; here the old ceramic warrior holds a weapon. The same technique could have been used to make a pick or club.

The Sweat Bath

The Nightfire Islanders, like virtually all western Indian, made use of another type structure, the sweat lodge. There were two types of these in existence at the time of European contact. The small family sweat lodge consisted of willows, bent over and draped with mats to contain the heated steam. The communal type was built more like a winter house but could not be dug deeply into the earth. It also had to be open on one side rather

Fig. 159. Basalt pick at bottom, and other basalt tools.

Fig. 160. The war club on this old Mexican statue suggests a method of wrapping basalt tools on a handle.

than at the top. Stones, weighing from three to five pounds, were heated in an outside fire, then passed through the opening to the interior where water was poured on them to generate steam. The earth-covered sweat lodge was probably the nearest thing to a religious structure in the Modoc culture. It served different purposes: as a place of purification following a funeral or for hunters preparing for a trip. Warriors and slavers readying themselves for a conquest could enjoy a session in the sweat lodge to purify themselves and bring good luck. Cleansing was incidental to the ceremonial function.

Considering that the only textiles available were made of tule or cattail fiber, and without towels or cloth, a method of getting dry after the sweat bath would seem difficult. Johnson discovered that the inventive Indians solved the problem by the use of sweat-scrapers made of bone, Figs. 161 and 162. Evidence shows that some were made with a perforation to wear around the neck; others were in simple spatula form. All have high polish from repeated use on the skins of the devoted bathers. Several fragments of sweat-scrapers were found on the floor of the burned sweat lodge by the University of Oregon scientific team. Another discovery was made because the charred rafters of the lodge were still preserved and in place, Fig. 163. Through the radio-carbon dating process, it was found that the building was about 1500 years old—the oldest known date for such a structure.

The Awesome Environment

If the sweat bath was the church of the Modoc, it certainly was not the only place where religion was practiced. Lives of the Modocs were so dominated by their religious beliefs that it is impossible to conceive, in our age of scientific enlightenment, the fears, superstitions and compulsions that governed them. The first and main element in their religion was a continuing effort to be at peace with their surroundings. The earth, the mountains, the springs—all were held in awe and reverence. In mythology, punishment by the spring, the earth or the cave is mentioned. This is understandable, considering the natural geological events that Modocs and their ancestors experienced. During the thousands of years they occupied the Klamath region, rapid changes took place in the earth's formations, changes that, even if the causes were known, would be terrifying to witness.

They saw violent eruptions nearby at Mount Lassen, which lies at the southern boundary of the Modoc range. This peak, now a national park, is still considered to be an active volcano. The earth boils and bubbles at "Bumpas Hell," Fig. 164, on the southern side of the mountain. Visitors are warned to keep away from the sulfurous springs.

The sight of snow-capped Mount Shasta must have fired the imaginations of the Modocs equally as much as it does the hikers and skiers of today. Shasta's towering heights completely dominated the scene at Nightfire village. East of the village, cinder cones were built and fiery lava coursed down the slopes like liquid tar in the Modoc Lava Beds. Mysterious caves and craters were left as the lava tubes became hollow from the outflow, Fig. 165. Such volcanic activity created earthquakes that must have shifted the block-fault mountains—at times shutting off the flow of precious springs, at times creating new ones.

In this fearsome environment, it is easy to understand the feelings of the Modocs and why they closely identified their religious activity with the earth, the mountains and the springs which surrounded them. Their chief and most powerful deity, Kmukamtch, was given credit for creating their universe and giving it to them.

Creation of the Modoc People

Indian tribes that have had a history of movement and travel usually have a legend relating to the migration. The Modoc people had occupied the Klamath highland for so many centuries that no migration myths existed. They did, though, have an explanation of the creation of their people and the neighboring Indians. Jeremiah Curtin was able to interview a Modoc informant, Koalakaka, who was exiled to Oklahoma following the Modoc War. Her version of creation was taken from the legend of

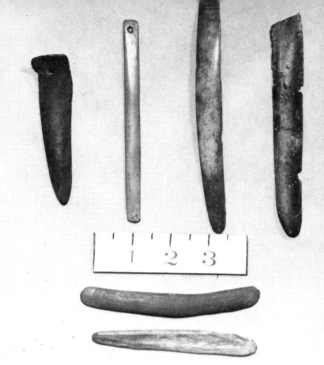

Fig. 161. Sweat scrapers with and without holes.

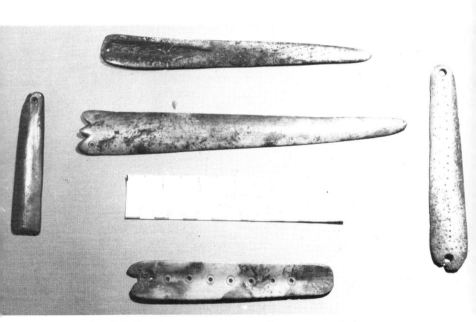

Fig. 162. Sweat scrapers were sometimes ornamented.

Fig. 163. Charred timbers of a 1500-year-old sweathouse are pointed out by an archaeology student.

Fig. 164. Mt. Lassen puts on a display at Bumpas Hell.

"Kmukamtch and His Daughter." Her comments regarding the Klamaths in this legend obviously reflect the troubled relationship that had existed between the Modocs and Klamaths prior to the Modoc War:

"Kmukamtch opened the basket and threw the bones in different directions. As he threw them, he named the tribe and kind of Indians they would be. When he named the Shastas he said: 'You will be good fighters.' To the Pit River and Warm Spring Indians he said: 'You will be brave warriors, too.' But to the Klamath Indians he said: 'You will be like women, easy to frighten.' The bones for the Modoc Indians he threw last, and he said to them: 'You will eat what I eat, you will keep my place when I am gone, you will be bravest of all. Though you may be few, even if many and many people come against you, you will kill them.' And he said to each handful of bones as he threw them: 'You must find power to save yourselves, find men to go and ask the mountains for help. Those who go to the mountains must ask to be made wise, or brave, or a doctor. They must swim in the gauwams and dream. When you are sure that a doctor has tried to kill someone, or that he won't put his medicine in the path of a spirit and turn it back, you will kill him. If an innocent doctor is killed, you must kill the man who killed him, or he must pay for the dead man.'

"Then Kmukamtch named the different kinds of food people should eat—catfish, salmon, deer and rabbit. He named more than two hundred different things, and as he named them they appeared in the rivers and the forests and the flats. He thought, and they were there. He said: 'Women shall dig roots, get wood and water and cook. Men shall hunt and fish and fight. It shall be this way in later times. This is all I will tell you.'

"When he had finished everything, Kmukamtch took his daughter and went to the edge of the world, to the place where the sun rises. He traveled on the sun's road till he came to the middle of the sky; there he stopped and built his house, and there he lives now."

Fig. 165. Lava flowed in the Modoc homeland as recently as 500 years ago.

Fig. 166. Horse Mountain Cave is marked by concentric circle petroglyph.

Weather—An Independent Force

Another force which bound the religious beliefs of the Modocs so closely to their surroundings was the connection between weather and the supernatural. Their legends give each natural phenomenon—such as wind, snow, thunder or rain—a personality and a power to affect the lives of the people. Animal gods, too, surrounded and, at times, were in competition with the chief god, Kmukamtch. In one legend recorded by Gatschet, the length of the winter was extended by the coyote trickster deity, Wash. She did this by hanging out twice as many moons as would normally appear during the winter months. Upon learning of this trick, Kmukamtch broke half of the moons, reducing the number of the winter months and the cold season. He also destroyed the coyote, Wash, by planting bone awls in the floor of her lodge, where she rolled upon them. Tctuk, the rock squirrel deity, was blamed for allowing snow to escape from the bag, thus creating the cold winters of the Klamath highland.

The Power Quest

The geographical world of the Modoc people was surrounded by mountains, caves and unusual-shaped rocks. These were often named after supernatural events and carried the power for good or evil over the lives of the residents. An event of great importance took place when a youngster reached adolescence; it was called the "power quest." Each person was thought to have a guardian spirit which was revealed to him in a dream or vision. The power quest journey usually took the adolescent to a mountain cave or cliff. The vision was actively sought by fasting and exercise.

Diving underwater, especially in an eel spring, was one method of seeking the dream. Piling rocks, especially along a cliff or rimrock, was frequently used as a way of searching for power. Many such rock cairns can still be found in the Klamath region. Probably fasting, and body neglect—even fever and delirium over a period of time—helped bring the dream of the animal, bird or object that was to help the individual achieve power over events in his future life.

One Modoc legend which, strangely enough, seems related to an actual geological feature, tells of the power quest of a Modoc girl who visited a cave on the fault-rim which separates the Tule Lake Basin from Lower Klamath Lake. It has been called "The Girl Saved by the Mountain." Curtin's version of the legend follows:

"There was a mountain between Tule and Klamath Lake; the top was smooth. On this mountain were swimming places and also a woman's medicine cave. . .Now a young girl just arriving at puberty went to this cave. Her mother told her she must tie a string around her waist, and when she got to the cave tie it to a strong bush so she could find her way out of the cave. There was a flat rock inside this cave, and on it were the marks of squirrel teeth. The girl was told that if she heard the teeth making a noise on the rock, she would know that she would be a great gambler. She was also told to pile up stones before going into this cave.

"The girl piled up stones, then tying the string to a bush and taking the other end in her hand, she entered the cave. While there she dropped the string and could not find it. She wandered five days and nights inside the cave; she was nearly starved and cried all the time. It was very dark. At last she fell over a rock. She got up, sat down and cried aloud. She slept and dreamed that someone told her to look up and see the stars. She woke and could see a little light over her head. That moment the rocks split open and made a path for her. She came out of the cave and went quickly home.

"The girl named the place where she came out "Waltoka." Her father had tried to go inside the cave in search of her but the rocks stood up in front of him like a wall and would not let him pass. The girl had gone in at Ufi Mountain but she came out far off. The mountain saved her."

An unusual circumstance, which seems to relate to this legend, occurred in 1976. The author was invited by Lava Beds National Monument Superintendent, Paul Haertel, to accompany Park,

Forest and Fish and Wildlife officials on a study of the area. The purpose was to plan boundary adjustments to improve visitor services of the agencies. One of the places visited was a cave on a mountainside containing a bedrock mortar on a flat rock with many small pits pecked around on the interior which had no apparent purpose. These small depressions made in the rock could have been a part of power quest activities. We shall never know for sure if this is the cave with the marks of squirrel teeth where the mountain saved the girl, but the cave will become a part of Lava Beds National Monument.

Rock Art

There are other cliffs and rimrocks where the rock cairns of the power quest can still be found. There are also certain caves and cliffs where carvings and paintings occur, some far from any camping place or spring. Others are virtually inaccessible and have no practical relationship with life-sustaining activity. The writer believes that many stone carvings were made as a part of the power quest.

The practice of making petroglyphs has great antiquity. The cave on Horse Mountain overlooking Clear Lake, Fig. 166, is an example of a cave that has not been used as a dwelling; nor is any water or foot nearby. The outside is marked by concentric circles; inside the walls are covered with geometric carvings, Fig. 167.

Some archaeologists feel that rock art has little or no meaning but rather represents doodling or aimless design by the makers. The fact that some of the designs appear more frequently lends credence to the belief that some message was intended. The design appearing most often is the concentric circle. The water bug, Fig. 168, is a design beautifully pecked high on a cliff not far from the Cradle Culture of Clear Lake. A similar carving also appears among the famous cliff carvings at Petroglyph Point in Modoc Lava Beds National Monument near Tulelake, California.

One cave in the Monument contains hundreds of both petroglyphs and the painted pictographs. The pictographs appear to be painted over the carvings and would therefore seem to be more recently made. One most interesting cave painting there shows a star inside a crescent moon. This has been interpreted by some as a representation of a super-nova which took place about the year 1,000. It is rare for Modoc pictographs to show the human form or animals. The "super kiuks" in Fig. 169 has four arms and is accompanied by a dog or coyote. The dotted lines probably had meaning to the dreamer who painted them.

There is so much reference to the power quest and cave visitations in the legends of the Modoc that those pictured in Fig. 170 are believed by the writer to be further evidence of this religious custom. Fortunately, the National Park Service has closed this cave until suitable supervision can be provided to prevent destruction of the primitive art.

The Indian method of passing along the legends and religious practices was by word of mouth around the winter-house fire or campfire. Modern-day ghost stories would be tame compared to the happenings in Modoc land—a land where everything in life had meaning. The powerful and frightening grip their beliefs held over the Modocs is illustrated by repeated references to the owl's hoot. This was an omen of death and caused those within proximity of the owl to flee in terror lest they be killed. Those who picked up a lark were said to become lazy and indolent.

All animals and fish had spirits, so hunters prepared themselves to deal with them in the proper way. Tools, weapons and implements also had spirits. Cressman reported visiting with a Klamath woman who talked lovingly to her two-horned wocas grinder as she prepared the lily seed.

The Henwas

The Modocs and Klamaths worshiped no idols and built no temples. The natural rocks, mountains and caves served them instead. They did, however, have one stone-sculptured piece of special importance and power. It was barely mentioned in Gatschet's Dictionary and was called a Hanuash, meaning "rock standing upright." When Dr. Roy Carlson served as curator of the Klamath County Museum, a group of such sculptured stones

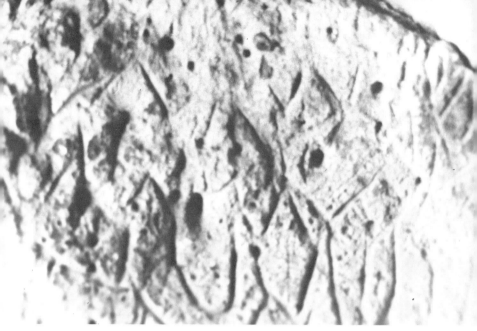

Fig. 167. Inside walls have numerous carvings in the rock.

Fig. 168. Water-bug petroglyph on rimrock near Clear Lake. (National Park Service)

Fig. 169. Human or animal figures are rare in Modoc art.

Fig. 170. Painted pictographs overlay older petroglyphs.

came to his attention. They were in the possession of a Klamath Indian woman, Lizzie Kirk.

Carlson made a special study of the rocks and then published an article in the *American Anthropologist*. This was the first description of the purpose and structure of these curious stones. He called them "henwas," a word easier to spell and pronounce than the original Indian word. Since the original Lizzie Kirk henwas were discovered and described, a few more have come to light, all in the territory of the Klamath Indians, none in Modoc territory. This in itself is unusual, as the Lutuami-speaking people shared most cultural traits. It would probably be an indication of more recent, but still prehistoric, development.

Of the new henwas revealed, seven are in the possession of Indian families. The author tried to buy one from an Indian lady who refused to sell it, saying: "They are good things to have." Those shown in Fig. 171, which I have called the Cascade Henwas, are owned by the Favell Museum in Klamath Falls. They were discovered in digging a building foundation at Johnson Prairie in the Cascade Mountains. They resemble human figures more than others.

There are a few characteristics common to most henwas. They are flat on the bottom to stand upright and usually they have lumps for arms. Some show female or male sex characteristics. Lizzie Kirk told Carlson that they had the power to travel underground or in the water and were used by the shamen. The stone figure found on Link River by Thomas Thomson, Fig. 172, probably represents the simplest form of henwas. It looks like a maul but has not been used on either end.

Another henwas that has come to light since Carlson's original description was found at Upper Klamath Lake on McCornack Point by Frank McCornack. This stone shows greater antiquity than most. One side was washed clean by the waves of the lake; the other has an accumulation of mineral where it was protected from the water. The McCornack henwas, Fig. 173, is larger than most; it weighs twenty-three pounds and is thirteen inches tall. It has the characteristic arms and even shows a tiny split or division at the top like the Chiloquin henwas.

The Yatish

None of the henwas stones with arms were found in the sands of Nightfire, as it was in Modoc country. Another type of sculptured stone, however, was discovered there, Fig. 174. This was in an early second-phase stratum well stained with "duck muck." Note that both stones shown had been broken. Other finds of these peculiarly shaped stones are referred to by collectors as: stirrup stones, medicine grinders, pile drivers, etc. No positive explanation of their use has ever been made. Most of the reported discoveries came from the older Lost River Cradle culture. A few were found in the territory of the Klamaths. However, they all have two common characteristics: they are flat on the bottom to make them stand upright, and they have indentations of equal depth on each side of the top part. Of the more than fifteen examined, few show signs of use either for pounding as a pile driver or for grinding as a small mortar.

The first clue to their purpose was found by the writer in Gatschet's Dictionary—"yatish," meaning "smaller rock standing upright." These stones, obviously much older than the henwas, fit the description perfectly. Two other clues are offered to substantiate ceremonial use of the stones. Fig. 175 shows three stones: one henwas and two yatish stones found together by Charlie Heaton on a hillside near Klamath Lake. They were probably used together.

The second clue to the mystery of the yatish was found by accident in the Jackson County Museum. Two stones were displayed there side by side, one a henwas, Fig. 176; the other, the familar stirrup-shaped stone obviously from a Modoc or Klamath prehistoric collection. My request for permission to photograph the henwas was granted through the courtesy of the museum director. I was also given the history of the two stones: They had been given to the museum by Alice Applegate Piel who, as a girl, had received them as a gift from the Indian woman who had taken

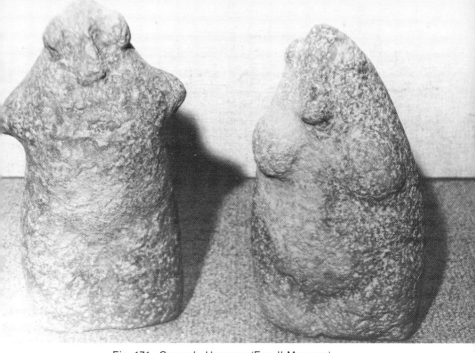

Fig. 171. Cascade Henwas. (Favell Museum)

Fig. 172. Link River Henwas.

Fig. 173. McCornack Henwas.

Fig. 174. Small rocks standing upright. Yatish?

care of her and the Applegate household at the Klamath Indian Sub-Agency headquarters. She was told of their value but did not realize what they were for.

When the family of Ivan Applegate left the Reservation, Alice was permitted to take the stones with her. As I was photographing the stones, I explained to the museum people that I wished to photograph only the henwas, as the other was not a henwas and was mislabeled. What I did not know, and what the Indian woman did know, as she gave her most prized possessions to the little girl, was that both stones had great power and were "good to have." One of these stones was a henwas, the other a yatish, "smaller stone standing upright."

During excavation at Nightfire, three complete yatish and three different broken yatish fragments were found, showing the culture trait to be common rather than an unusual occurrence during the early part of the second phase. Another early-period stone in the center of Fig. 177 appears to be an unfinished yatish in the process of manufacture. The stone on the left side of the figure is from Lost River near Bonanza; the one on the right is from Clear Lake, both in the Cradle Culture.

Mourning Customs

Death was never far away from the people of Nightfire, and infant mortality must have been exceedingly high. There were no antibiotics, no surgeons, and the only milk available was mother's milk. Added to this was the constant threat of raids and counter raids. An account given by Sergeant Morgan, an Indian informant, recreates a picture of the tension under which the Modoc lived, as well as the funeral customs of the time: "All night long screeches the big owl presaging people die." After this bad omen, the village was raided by armor-wearing warriors. Burning the lodges and killing the occupants, they allowed one man to escape in the water. He reached the village of his relatives, who assembled a group to attack the raiding party. Morgan said that five were killed on one side and many on the other, and the raiders were dispersed.

After the battle, the fallen defenders were gathered. Limbs of trees and brush were carried to build a funeral pyre. The body of the warrior was placed upon the pyre and in Morgan's words: "They then fired it, the whole they fired. Cast into it they his quiver. Sorrowfully wept they in mourning; at his death they wept. Now that whole body was burned up; then they all returned from cremating. They went back to homes and cut off the hair of his wife, who was widowed. Resin [pine pitch] she laid on her head because widowed, then went sweating. Five days she sweated; then returned home, and fish ate. That's the end."

The widow's duties involved three things: placing pitch on the head, five days of sweat baths, and then the fish diet.

Skull Trophies

Mortuary practices were obviously not the same for all the dead, judging from the observations of fur-trader Peter Skene Ogden. His party of Hudson's Bay Company trappers, with their families and horses, had just finished the difficult trip through the Snake country of Eastern Oregon on December 12, 1826. On this day he wrote in his Journal:

"We saw five Huts of Indians who had collected around their Huts no small quantity of Small Fish for their winter store. . . Happy race whose wants are so few and live happy and contented with such miserable food and I may add live and die independent of others. In my travels last year I observed the Clammettee (Klamath) Nation and what not only surprised me but what appeared most strange, was to see within ten yards of their Huts three skulls and within nearly as short a distance of another Hut I saw two, nor did they appear of a very old date. This is as it ought to be—the living and the dead remain together and acts as a warning to them that sooner or later they must also die."

The skulls he observed were thought to be trophies brought home for use in the victory dance. Unlike their cousins, the Klamaths, the Modocs had no fixed period of waiting before cremation took place. Over more than six thousand years their practice of caring for the dead changed during different periods. In some

Fig. 175. Heaton Henwas with yatish.

Fig. 176. Applegate Henwas.
(Jackson County Museum)

Fig. 177. Cradle Culture yatish with unfinished Nightfire stone.

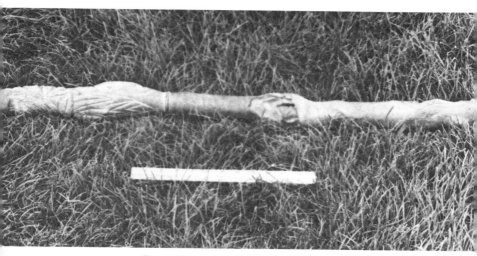

Fig. 178. The Charlie Cowan medicine-wand.

cases, it appeared that "who you were" and "what you owned" made a difference in the type of funeral provided.

Paint Deposits

When excavations were first undertaken at Nightfire, there were several burials in phase three of occupation but no evidence of burials or cremation in the two earliest phases of the island midden. Scattered pieces of human skeletal material in the lower levels suggested that there was little regard for the dead and no ceremony. A fortunate circumstance later proved that this reasoning was wrong. When an irrigation ditch was cut near the west side of the island to carry water to a nearby field, the ditching blade came out covered with a bright scarlet color.

Investigation showed an amazing funeral practice that had been unknown in Modoc customs. Here on a level conforming with the earliest period of occupation were several accumulations of burned human bones. They occurred in deposits containing the charred remains of one, two or even three individuals. The small size of the material and the mixture of ash clearly showed that cremation had taken place at another site, perhaps on the main island of Sheepy Ridge. The remains were then carried to the west side of Nightfire. Some deposits were heavily mixed with a scarlet ochre paint; others contained only ash, charcoal and bones. There were few funeral offerings in the deposits but enough to reveal much about the first migrants to Nightfire.

Why had these early people transported the burned remains to a different place? The lack of fuel for cremation seems an obvious reason for burning the dead at another site. Although it is doubtful that Sheepy Ridge ever supported a forest, there would have been a continuous supply of sagebrush, which burns with an intense heat.

The custom of mixing human bone fragments with ochre before deposit occurred also in phase two on the island. The purpose of mixing the bones with the ochre is unknown. It has been suggested that the red paint represented the replacement of human blood. The use of ground-mineral paint must have been widespread as the word for ochre, k'lepski, was in common use in the Klamath language. The red color was evidently obtained by burning yellow ochre.

A feature which occurred in every paint lens discovered in the phase-two midden of Nightfire was the presence of at least one rock. This was sometimes a crude pestle or maul, usually just a stone. One such deposit contained three bone beads. Their unsmoothed condition shows that they had never been worn but were evidently made purposely to place in the deposit.

Smoking-pipes in the third and later phases were sometimes associated with cremations or burials, but the presence of these or other objects of value seemed to depend more upon the status of the deceased and the wealth of the mourners than on any fixed custom. The early-period cremations at Nightfire seemed to contain only those objects worn by the deceased, or nothing at all. It was customary in the nineteenth century for the plateau Lutuami-speaking people to destroy the worldly goods of the dead at the time of cremation.

The frequent occurrence of single human bones disassociated with other skeletal material was to be expected. The writer does not believe that finding them among cooking rocks on house floors or along with other debris is a sign of cannibalism. The site had been occupied for so many centuries that the digging of house pits, cooking pits, and the wave action of the lake during periods of high water would all have had a tendency to stir up the contents of the soil and disperse it along with the rocks.

The Shaman or Kiuks

A Modoc doctor was a Kiuks; the name was taken from the sign hung over their lodge on a oblique pole. The sign could be a rabbit skin or other animal skin to let the populace know that the medicineman was in and ready for practice. Indians reported that the Kiuks, or medicinemen, not only treated the sick but also presided over the communal dances, provided consultant service on dreams, predicted the weather, and during various gathering activities gave the signal for the beginning of the harvest. As a badge of their profession, some were said to wear a high leather hat.

Kiuks had specialities and each had his own messenger to communicate with the gods. Some used the weasel or mink. The crane, frog and spider were also used, according to the dream or vision that the practicioner had undergone in the process of passing the test and qualifying as a conjurer. Both men and women practiced medicine. In the year 1888, it was estimated that more women than men were in the Kiuks business on the Klamath Reservation.

Some doctors were greatly feared because of their power to cast spells or bewitch others. In treating the sick, a chant or song was given, calling upon a certain animal or curing tool to come to the patient and remove the cause of the disease. Charlie Cowan, a Modoc Indian, showed the author a carved wand, Fig. 178, which he found in the Modoc Lava Beds in 1931 while herding sheep there. He said that it was a medicineman's wand or scepter and it gave him an eerie feeling to hold it. Poor Charlie may have been right. He led an unfortunate life and was later killed.

In examining the buried archaeological specimens of a vanished people, it is easy to let the imagination replace sound judgment or proved scientific information. Pioneer archaeologists were occasionally inclined to label an unknown stone or art object as a ceremonial piece. At the risk of falling into this common error, the writer believes there were two deposits buried in the soils of Nightfire that were formerly the possessions of Indian shamen. One sugh deposit found in the phase-three level included the giant shoulderblade of a buffalo, Fig. 179. The size of the animal can be estimated by comparing it with the scapula taken from a male three-point mule deer shown in the upper part of the figure. A local butcher said that the bone was larger than those found in most cattle—probably the same size as the bones in the largest bulls.

Buried with the bison bone were a number of large birdbones. The top one in Fig. 179 has been perforated by rubbing so that it

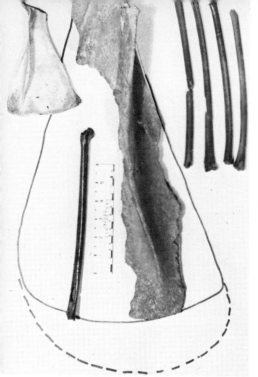

Fig. 179. Giant buffalo bone buried with a set of waterfowl bones.

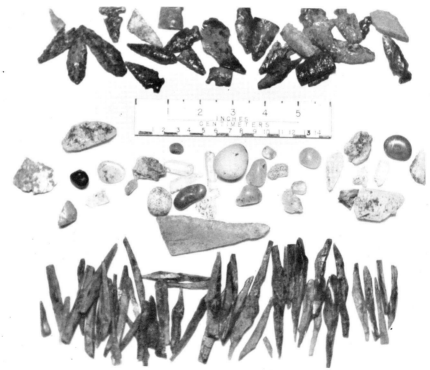

Fig. 180. An unusual deposit of obsidian splinters, colored stones and old projectile points.

could have been used as a whistle; however, the hole may have been created unintentionally. Other waterfowl bones in this burial appear to have been rubbed, but not enough to wear through the bone. These bone objects, which were found together with shellbeads, could, of course, have been the trophies of a hunter, but their use as curing tools seems more likely. Another deposit found in the same age level included all the stones in Fig. 180. The most amazing part of this prehistoric cache is the group of forty-three obsidian, needle-like formations shown at the bottom of the picture. These are sometimes called bangles by archaeologists. They were not shaped or manufactured by the Indians but are the products of nature. The nearest natural occurrence of these strange formations is in Plum Valley, halfway between Lakeview, Oregon, and Alturas, California. Rockhounds also report them at Glass Butte between Bend and Burns in Central Oregon. The finding of single splinters of obsidian in Indian sites is not especially rare but finding such a large number indicates that their possession by a single owner is unusual. The agate, crystal and colorful rock collection in the cache included thirty-one stones. It must have required a lifetime to gather them as none of the specimens are to be found in the vicinity of Nightfire Island. Some appear to have been traded from the coast; others are to be found in the territory of the Shasta Indians in the Siskiyou Mountains.

The twenty-seven chipped pieces in the cache are mostly of obsidian but include a few colorful, broken fragments. The workmanship indicates that different knappers made the assortment. Both percussion and pressure flaking were used in their manufacture. Most of the pieces were originally made for projectile points, but drills, gravers and a small blade can be seen in the collection. None of the points are Gunther-type—which is the predominant type found after the bow and arrow came into use.

What does this collection mean? We shall never know for sure, but we can be certain that it was an unusual occurrence. Drawing from the primitive priesthood, it is possible to recreate a scene where the shaman calls forth the magic of these crystals: He has arranged them before an audience held in hypnotic attention by his chants and movements. Most likely the occasion was for the healing of the sick. In such case, a chorus of female chanters would answer the incantations of the doctor. The ceremony could, however, have been in preparation for a raid, in which case the spirit of the magic crystals or the ancient points would have been called forth to protect the young braves and bring them home laden with bounty. Or, the setting might have been a ceremony prior to an encounter with one of the grizzly bears— whose bones and teeth are contained in the ancient strata of the village.

A different scene might have involved the removal of a curse or evil spirit from an unfortunate victim—inflicted by a vengeful shaman of a different village. Such an array of medical tools would be much more impressive than the simple couch of today's psychiatrists or the thermometer and stethoscope of the physician.

In the Modoc culture the shamen occupied a position of power even greater than that of the village leader. They could arouse the fear and respect of the community, demand tribute and accumulate great wealth. The profession, however, had one great disadvantage. If the songs and curing tools did not restore the patient's health, and death resulted from the treatment, the relatives could—under the rules and customs—demand that the doctor be killed.

Congenital Defect at Nightfire

One of the investigators on the scientific team assembled for the 4-SK-4 study was Dr. Kenneth A. Bennett, a physical anthropologist. He examined the skeletal materials gathered by Johnson and reported that health conditions in the village during the fourth phase must have been generally poor and unusual in one respect. He noted in the *American Journal of Physical Anthropology*, May 1972, that nine of the ten skeletons examined had evidence of sacral rachischisis, a failure of the spinal vertebrae to close (also known as spina bifida). Bennett attributed this unusual proportion of the disease to the inbreeding in a remote, small, isolated village.

Lucky Stones

While the occurrence of such a large deposit of agates and stones is unusual, the possession of a single agate was rather common for the Nightfire people, especially during the last four thousand years of occupation. The presence of these stones in funerary offerings indicates that they meant more to the owner than just pretty rocks.

Indians of the southwestern United States and northern Mexico collected crystals and odd mineral formations in the belief that they had been formed by lightning or other "supernatural" events. These possessions were kept in the medicine bag and highly prized because it was felt that they imparted power to the owner. The Modocs, too, gathered or traded for a wide variety of unusual rocks.

Fig. 181 shows a sampling of such items. None of these are found in the geologic formations of the Modoc homeland except possibly the fossil. The numbers in the figure indicate the following: 1. agate, 2. unusual concretion, 3. crevice quartz, 4. part of a fossil horsetooth, 5. quartz crystals, 6. calcite crystal, 7. felspar. The pieces in the upper part of the figure are various types of petrified wood. Two of these show signs of wear as though they had been used as paint palettes. If these formations were to be given a modern name, it would probably be lucky stones or power stones. They might bring protection, power or luck in gambling or in hunting.

Another object that was said to bring good luck, according to Gatschet, was the left hind leg of a frog. The finding of an old stone arrowhead was also a lucky omen. Too bad that these unenlightened people did not know about a rabbit's foot.

Raids and Warfare

Historically, the Modocs established a reputation for aggressive behavior. Even before the Modoc War, a traveler through Yreka

Fig. 181. A varied assortment collected by ancient rockhounds.

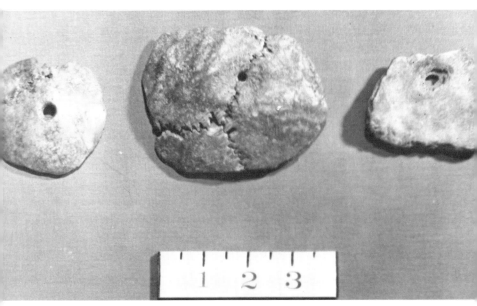

Fig. 182. Trophy pendants made from human skulls.

called them the "lordly Modoc." A brief glance into the past was given the author in 1968. It was in Lassen National Park and Mrs. Selinda La Marr, a Hot Creek (Atsugewi) Indian, had just finished a demonstration on basket weaving. Seeking to establish a friendly relationship with her, I mentioned that I had some friends who were Modocs. She turned around and refused to speak or look at me. Scene two took place two years later at the same location. I asked Mrs. La Marr if she knew anything about the Modoc Indians. Her answer: "They used to come at night to kill people in their beds." I had known that the Modoc raids ranged into the territory of the Shastas but did not realize that they had reached the Hat Creek region.

Paul Schultz, author, said that the Modocs were traditional enemies of the Atsugewi, who had prepared places for defense in case of raids. The Pit River (Achomawi) and the Shastas, who bordered Modoc country, were even more often participants in these continuing conflicts. The Modocs, who told Verne Ray about methods of warfare, agreed with Mrs. La Marr that raiding, rather than formal battle, was preferred. Slave trading was usually the principal purpose but scalps and whole heads were sometimes taken.

The Nightfire Island warriors were evidently successful in returning with heads as the skull pendants testify, Fig. 182. These were found at an early occupation level about 5,000 B.P., before trade in shell beads was started. The one at the right has been nicely finished. The other two have been drilled and shaped with some rounding of the edge but are hardly suitable for ornaments. Two other examples have been found in the territory of the Modoc. The skull trophy in Fig. 183 was discovered by Burt Thomas on the dry lakebed of Lower Klamath before the bird refuge was established. It also appears to have great age and is nearly fossilized. It is hard to account for the strange pieces of neckwear except to conclude that they were trophies—perhaps stone-age status symbols to compare with the wearing of scalps by the Plains Indians, or feather coups to indicate bravery in battle.

Fig. 183. This skull pendant appears to be fossilized.

Fig. 184. Deerhoof rattles accompanied the dance.

Archaeologists tend to be quite critical of the theories of their
fellows. Most are even reluctant to guess about the unproved
materials of their profession. But for the layman, with no scientific reputation to protect, it is easier to propose solutions to unanswered questions. Knowledge of the fierce character of the
Modocs makes it easier to explain the mystery of the skull pendants. According to their own accounts and those of their enemies,
the Modocs were both aggressive and successful in warfare, but at
Nightfire there was proof that sometimes a price was paid. Johnson found the skeletons of two young warriors without heads.
Both had arrowpoints in the skeletal structure, likely put there by
Shastas on a revenge raid.

The Dance

If the ancient soils of Nightfire produced more evidence of the
bad times than the good, this does not mean that there were no
good times. Story telling and gambling were popular, and there
was also evidence of the dance. Dancing among the Modocs,
though, did not reach the development of complex patterns such
as those of Plains or Southwest Indians. Neither were the dances
such great social occasions as those of other Northern California
tribes. There were, however, several kinds of Modoc dances. One
was a dance of incitement to battle or war prior to a raid. Another was a dance held after a successful raid—a hair dance or scalp
dance—where occasionally fur from various animals was added
to human tropies on the scalp pole. Gatschet has described the
scalp dance as it was related to him by the Modocs:

"This scalp-dance tune is one of the many heard at these dances
during the earlier Modoc wars. A peeled tree, sometimes twenty
feet high, was planted into the ground, otter and rabbit skins
fastened on or near the top, and below them the scalps of the
enemy killed in battle. Forming a wide ring around this pole
(walash), the tribe danced, stood or sat on the ground, looking
sometimes at solitary dancers; moving and yelling (yaka) around
the pole at others who tried to shake it, or at fleet horses introduced to run inside the ring."

Another traditional dance activity was sponsored by every family, according to Ray's informants. They held a "coming out" party or puberty dance for their girls. One of the purposes was to announce their availability for marriage. The social event was so universal that if a girl lacked a family, arrangements were made by friends. Time and the elements have erased the remains of any dance rattles at Nightfire. The deer-hoof rattles in Fig. 184 were used in the puberty dances of the Klamaths.

A dance common to tribes along the Klamath River, and in the region of Humboldt Bay, was the obsidian dance, according to A.L. Kroeber, who studied these people in great depth. The central theme of the ceremony was to bring these precious knives from their hiding places upon the orders of the village elders. After brandishing them in their tribal dances to impress the neighbors and to establish their own prestige, the owners returned the big obsidian pieces to their secret hiding places until further dancing was announced.

Portions of these large knives have been found in the Klamath Basin and eastward. Like their neighbors down-river, the men of Nightfire evidently took part in the obsidian blade dance. Up until now, no one has known how long ago this tradition started. Three different fragments, Fig. 185, were found and one was sent for dating. Obsidian hydration tests made at the University of Oregon have shown that the blades were about 1500 years old. The large blade at the bottom of the figure has been notched, possibly for wearing as an ornament or in a dance. The fragments on the right of the figure are from a much larger blade, more like those in the territory of the Yurok and Hupa.

No fragments of the large ceremonial blades were found in the first three phases at Nightfire. Since the only established date is 1,500 B.P., it is hard to tell if the obsidian dance originated in the Great Basin or down-river with the Shastas, Hupas or Yuroks.

Woman Power

Much of Modoc mythology concerns one animal deity or another taking the form of man and attempting to steal the wife of

Fig. 185. Obsidian dance-knife and fragments.

Fig. 186. Enormous pile of wocas bulbs demonstrated woman power.

another. From the standpoint of pure economics, this practice would make sense. Modoc Indian society ran on woman power, though perhaps not as much at Nightfire Island where hunting and fishing were so important, as in other villages where seeds and roots provided the sustenance. But even here there were hides to be tanned, baskets to be woven, endless garments to be made, and tule shoes and feather blankets to be furnished. Grandmothers did much of the child care while mothers brought in the burden baskets filled with camas, duck eggs and wocas. There were times when women were forbidden to touch their hair with their fingers and they had to use a head-scratcher. Other restrictions and taboos made them live alone at times. Girls at puberty had to perform exhausting tasks. The enormous pile of wocas pods in Fig. 186 is an example of woman's work. The processing and grinding had only begun.

Even though women were permitted to become conjurers and doctors, and they provided the mainstay of their family, their status was very low—little better than slavery—probably more like property. There is some evidence of a "bride price" being paid in the stone-age wedding arrangements, but no surety that the practice was always followed. Early informants indicated that the value of gifts given for the bride insured her status in the village. Myrtle Caldwell's great-grandmother, a Happy Camp Karok, was sold to a Dutchman named Billings. Mrs. Caldwell said that she thought this practice was common; her family even had some pride in the fact that she was so desirable. Her success and happiness as a wife and mother proved that in this case the matrimonial arrangement worked.

In some Indian societies, the groom went to live with the parents of the bride; in others, the bride left her family to live in the village of the male. The maul in Fig. 187 offers evidence of the latter custom prevailing. The one at right is a plain fourth-phase maul; the other shows a distinct ring around the base. This is characteristic of the Shasta or Lower River Indians.

David Cole, University of Oregon archaeologist, said that certain customs of a people can be discovered by the type of outside

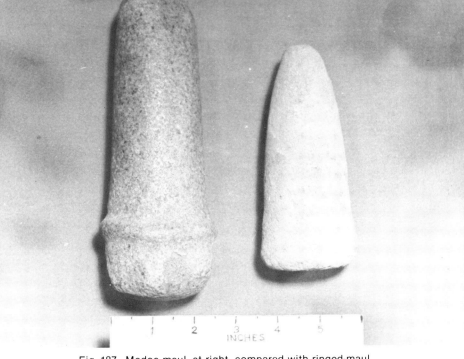

Fig. 187. Modoc maul, at right, compared with ringed-maul
from the Lower River.

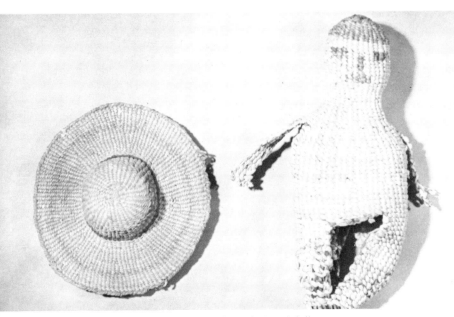

Fig. 188. Toy basketry hat and doll.

goods brought in. If a new variety of weapons is introduced, it indicates that the male went to live with the parents of the bride. If women's tools, representing a foreign material culture, are introduced, the likelihood is that the bride was brought home by the husband. The maul pictured could have been the result of a slave raid, but it seems unlikely that a captive would either desire or be permitted to bring her favorite meat-pounder along. More likely it is an indicator of a voluntary union. It seems certain that no outside weapon-makers came to live at Nightfire, as styles of projectile points hardly changed for 4,000 years—not until the introduction of the bow and arrow.

Toys and Games

Hunting and fishing occupied most of the time of the men on Nightfire Island. Root digging, weaving and cooking occupied the women. The only school was the family. A glimpse of this life was obtained by Ida Momyer Odell, who spent her early childhood at the Klamath Indian Reservation where the Klamaths, Modocs and Yahooskin Snakes were living after the Modoc War. It is fortunate that she had a sense of history being made; also an urge to serve her fellow citizens. She was active in forming the first Klamath County Historical Society and in pushing for the founding of a museum. A glimpse of the Indian women of the time was provided by Mrs. Odell in an interview with the author. She said that the Indian women were very kind and loving. They would join in visiting and twining baskets and would allow her to do some of the twining. However, Mrs. Odell felt sure that it was necessary afterwards for them to remove all that she had done and then start the basket where they had left off.

The basketry doll, Fig. 188, is an example of a girl's toy. Another doll, Fig. 189, made of cloth, was found in a cave in what is now the Lava Beds National Monument before the monument was founded. Most likely the doll was left when the Modoc warriors and their families escaped through the barricades during the night. The doll was given to Mrs. Odell, who passed it along with many other mementos of the Indians, so that the descendants of

Fig. 189. Rag doll found in
Modoc Lava Beds.

Fig. 190. Stone balls, at top, from Casa Grandes, Mexico. The ones at the
bottom are from Nightfire.

these durable people, as well as the public, can view a part of their heritage in the Klamath County Museum. Little girls played with dolls, baskets and the babies of the village. Little boys shot at each other with arrows made of rye grass, according to Modoc informants. These youngsters had to learn to speak the Lutuami language, which had a vocabulary of about 24,000 words, but no written language.

There is evidence that the Nightfire Modoc participated in a form of entertainment which was widespread among American Indians—playing with stone balls, Fig. 190. The Lutuami-speaking people had a word, "kolkoli," meaning "ball made for playing." The round stones at the bottom of the picture are from the third and fourth phases, making them range from 4,000 years B.P. An Indian informant told Alfred Collier that the ballgame was played by bowling the stones at holes in the ground in order to see who could get the ball to enter the hole with the least number of attempts. The winner was determined by low score as in today's golf. The round balls at the top of Fig. 190, a little larger and more carefully rounded, are from the Casa Grandes culture in Chihuahua, Mexico. Though it does not seem unusual to find stone balls in another Indian culture, what does seem unusual is that the game, described by the informant in Mexico, was virtually the same game as described to Mr. Collier.

Some games were reserved for women. One of these consisted of casting marked beaver teeth or woodchuck teeth onto a stone grinding slab (metate). The winner was decided by the combination of marks turning up after the teeth or dice had been cast. Scores were kept by twelve painted sticks, called checks, which were stuck into the ground in front of the winner. When all twelve checks were obtained by one winner, the game ended.

For Modoc men, gambling was by far the most popular form of recreation. They played the stick game, as did most other western Indians. They gambled for high stakes, at times even risking wives and daughters, but beads provided the most popular stakes. To obtain these beads, they were dependent on trade with Indians of the coast and the Siskiyou Mountains region.

8. TRADE AND COMMERCE

Despite the raiding, slaving and enmity that existed between Modocs and the river tribes, tradegoods from the coastal region shows that all relations were not on a warlike basis. Seashell beads appeared in the early second phase, about five thousand years ago, and did not lose their popularity even after the introduction of European glass beads. In fact, the first copper beads were rolled in imitation of dentalium. It seems strange that the Nightfire people placed little value on local shells for ornamental purposes. A few beads of freshwater mussels were found in the Cradle Culture at Clear Lake but the shells must have been too common to be used extensively.

At Nightfire village, mussel shells were found during the third phase as illustrated in Fig. 191. The largest of the three deposits, shown in the lower part of the figure, contained 203 beads. Those grouped in the middle have irregular shapes and are unusual in that they have been drilled with the circle-and-dot technique, which was normally used only to decorate bone objects. All of these thin white disks are larger than the common disks cut from olivella shell.

Pacific Coast Contact

At the time the pioneer Modocs left the dried shores of Lower

Fig. 191. Thin shells of local molluscs were seldom used.

Fig. 192. Antler tools for fleshing and tanning hides.

Klamath Lake to establish a new campsite on Sheepy Creek, there was little evidence of trade with other tribes. Shortly after this, about 7,000 radio-carbon years before the present, a few trade items started to appear, suggesting contact with the Pacific Coast. First, there were plain olivella shells with the spire ground off. We shall never know for sure if some adventurous Modoc group traveled to the coast to gather the shells or if they were traded from down-river residents.

Not too many centuries later, the shells of dentalium appeared and continued to show in the sediments of the island throughout its occupation. We can be sure the appearance of dentalium proves trade with other Indians. Not only was the distance too great for the Modocs to travel to obtain these shells but a highly specialized technique was required to catch these molluscs from the ocean floor.

As time passed, a greater variety of tradegoods appeared— haliotis shell and clam, colored sandstone and clay, precious jade, soapstone and serpentine from the deep canyon of the Klamath River, and precious crystals and agates from the limestone region south of Mount Shasta. Did the Modocs trade for the unfinished stone, then finish it themselves, or did they trade for the finished ornaments of steatite and serpentine? We shall never know for sure.

We shall also never know how many hands the merchandise passed through before reaching Nightfire Island, nor what the price markup was each time it changed hands. The trade pattern seems to have been southwest down the Klamath River rather than toward the Columbia or the Sacramento Valley. We do know that commerce was established by the Modoc with the Wasco Indians on the Columbia in later times, but this was near the time of the historic period.

Each year archaeological evidence is discovered; then a time lag occurs before it reaches print. At this writing, there seems to be no evidence to show that the northwest California coast was occupied during the period more than 2,000 years ago. The primitive tradegoods at Nightfire indicates that new discoveries will show occupation and trade much earlier.

Modoc Trade Goods

In order to trade, both parties must be satisfied that they have made a good exchange. What, then, would the Nightfire Islanders have to offer in order to get the coastal or Lower River Indians to part with their precious shells—steatite and jade? What could they afford to part with that would not cause them to be deprived of necessary things? The commodity they would have in the greatest amount would have been dried duckmeat, perhaps ground into pemmican with dried berries. Wocas seeds would be easy to transport but the stone industry does not support the idea that wocas was widely used.

One commodity the Modocs could claim was obsidian in great quantities. Arrowpoints in the Sacramento Valley and much of Northern California show that Glass Mountain material was used in their manufacture. Some of the giant blades of the Humboldt region and the Rogue River Shasta were made from Glass Mountain obsidian. According to Heizer, the North Sacramento Wintu split chunks from the large blocks at Glass Mountain by building a fire against the obsidian. Did the Modocs sell it, exact tribute for it, or assume it was put there by Kmukamtch for everyone to use?

The woman power and perhaps slave power of the Nightfire Islanders could produce another product in quantities for export —animal skins and basketry. Bone counts show that the hunters were skilled in getting large game. The tanned skins would have been an excellent trade item for the fishing people who were their neighbors down-river. The antler tools shown in Fig. 192 were most likely used for cleaning the flesh from hides and working them into a suitable condition for tanning. A polish shows on the ends even after years in the soil. Both the curve of the antler and its length made it suitable for use in wedges. Since they occur at all levels of the midden—some as fragments—a continuous use for hide dressing is suggested.

Fig. 193. Elkhorn spoon with other antler tools.

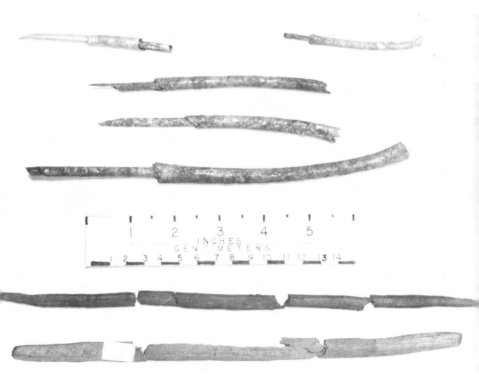

Fig. 194. At top, bones within bones. At bottom, long slender objects of antler.

Fig. 195. A wide variety of ocean shells reached Nightfire.

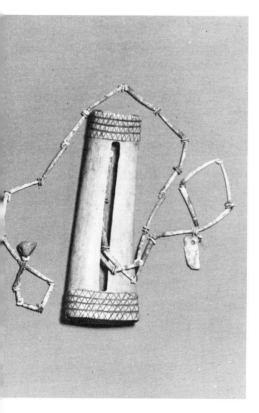

Fig. 196. Yurok elkhorn purse with "alkelchik" beads.

Bone Tools

The large mammals of the Modoc area provided another product for export—bone tools. Tools of elkhorn are shown in Fig. 193. The two at the bottom are slender scoop-shaped tools, their purpose unknown. Next above is a thin elkhorn spoon, quite different from the fancy ornamented spoons made by the tribes along the lower part of the Klamath River. The four antler objects in the upper part of the figure have rounded ends rather ' than pointed. They are different from most arrow-flakers.

Another group of bones for which no purpose is known is shown at the top of Fig. 194. They are birdbones with other birdbones inserted in them. Such combinations are quite common in the midden of Modoc sites. A few show that the smaller bone has been sharpened to a point. In most cases the bones are not straight enough to be used as an arrowshaft. For lack of a better name, I have called them "marrow pickers." The long, narrow elkhorn pieces at the bottom of the figure also defy a proper explanation of purpose. I have wondered if they could have been inserted in the warp in the process of weaving feather blankets.

Medium of Exchange

Marine shells made into beads or ornaments provided the single best medium of exchange in the age of barter. The traders of Nightfire were successful in acquiring the greatest variety of shells reported on any site. In Fig. 195, ten different species are shown by number: 1. dentalium, 2. three sizes of olivella, 3. cut haliotis, 4. cut clamshell, 5. a thinner species of clam, 6. clam, 7. mussel, 8. limpet, 9. keyhole limpet, 10. unknown bivalve, 11. glycimerous. The rarest shellbeads at Nightfire were the glycimerous and limpet. It is questionable if the marine mussel shells in number 7 were ever made into beads. Why they were taken over the long, dangerous journey up the Klamath River to the Great Basin remains a mystery.

All kinds of shellbeads were prized by the American Indians, but the favorite in the West was the dentalium. The wealth-loving Yurok on the coast invented a special purse made of hollowed elkhorn to hold these shells, Fig. 196. These tooth-like shells were gathered off the coast of Vancouver Island by the Nootkas. They were then traded down the coast and up the Klamath River to reach the island of 4-SK-4. They provided the nearest thing to a medium of exchange among the Northwest Indians. Kroeber said: "As might be expected, the value of dentalia was greater in California than among the tribes at the source of supply. In Washington or Northern Oregon a slave was rated at a string; but the northern string was a fathom long. Among the Nootka, money was still cheaper; it took five fathoms to buy a slave." The length of the individual shell had great bearing upon its value. Shorter shells like those in the necklace in Fig. 197 had less value. Some were delicately carved to add to the desirability.

Dentalium shells never reached a state of abundance among the Modocs. Indications are that they were used sparingly, some as sequins rather than beads. The names "alkelchik" and "tutash" were both Indian words used to describe the shells. Evidence indicates that other styles of beads were usually mixed with the tooth-shaped dentalia. Modocs were also known sometimes to wear dentalium in the septum of the nose, as a matter of fashion.

By far the most numerous beads at Nightfire were the olivella shells. They were also the first marine shells to appear—about 5,500 years ago in phase one. In order to make a bead from the natural shell of olivella, it was necessary only to grind the end from the spire of the shell on an abrasive stone. The other kinds of beads were cut from these popular shells: the half olivella in Fig. 198, row 5, and the disk beads in rows 2, 3 and 4.

The shells from three different species of clams appear in Nightfire deposits, but surprisingly there were none of the thick, disk clamshell beads so popular in the Sacramento Valley. The absence of these beads and of charm stones leads to the belief that Modocs did not carry on trade with Indians in the Sacramento drainage basin.

In terms of age, the shells of the clam appear to have arrived at 4-SK-4 after the olivella and dentalium, about the same time as the haliotis. Kroeber said, "The Yurok obtained the haliotis or

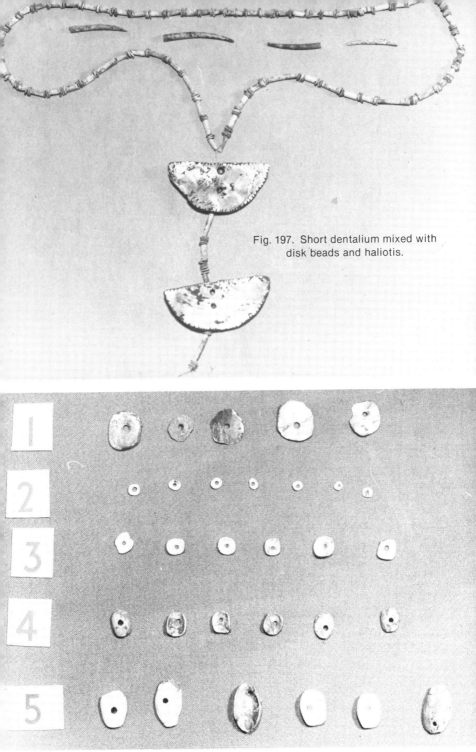

Fig. 197. Short dentalium mixed with disk beads and haliotis.

Fig. 198. Five types of disk beads.

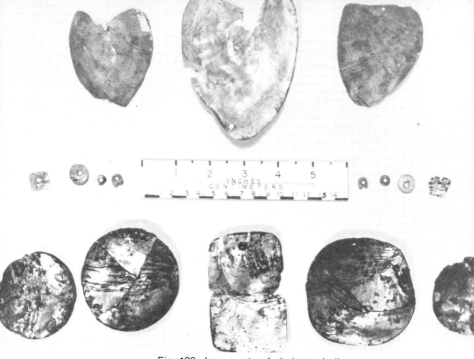

Fig. 199. Large cuts of abalone shell.

Fig. 200. Shiny bone pendant with beads reworked from haliotis disks.

abalone shells near Cape Mendocino." It appears that two different species of haliotis were used. All of the objects in Fig. 199
are made from the shell of these two species. The great contrast in
size is shown by the picture. The largeness of some pieces indicates that value was placed upon mass as well as artistry.

The fact that all the large pieces were perforated for stringing
does not necessarily mean that they were worn about the neck. It
is hard to imagine a world without pockets; yet, if you have
neither jacket nor pants, you have no place for pockets. Many
objects used by primitive people were drilled for attachment to a
string or cord simply because this was a way to carry them. A skin
bag, of course, served also to make up for the absence of pockets.

The haliotis beads in Fig. 200 have been cut from larger pendants, such as those shown in the previous figure. Most of them retain some of the circular shape of the original rim. Many show
double perforations which, no doubt, would keep the beads from
slipping on the sinew or cord of the necklace. The highly polished
bone piece found with the beads is eleven centimeters (4½ inches)
long, so could have served as an ornament, head-scratcher or
sweat-scraper. Some of the ribbon-like haliotis pendants at the
top of Fig. 201 have been carved to enhance their beauty, while
three of those at the bottom of the picture show multiple perforations as though they served as a point of attachment for other
bangles or ornaments.

The broad, flat haliotis shell allowed the beadmaker to exercise
greater imagination than when using the smaller mollusks. In
Fig. 202 a number of different shaped cuts are shown. The larger
pendants at the bottom are about 2½ inches long.

Beads of Bone

Shellbeads of the various mollusks are sometimes strung in
strands of a single species and occasionally mixed. They were at
times mixed with beads and bones. Those in Fig. 203 have been
arranged to illustrate the way they were strung to form an apron.
The birdbone tubes have not been well finished, only cut enough

to make them break into the proper length. The shells, interspersed with the birdbones, are a larger type of olivella. The lower rectangular cuts of haliotis were found in a large group in the late fourth phase. The apron is patterned after an illustration by Dixon of a Shasta apron.

In contrast to the poorly finished birdbone tubes in the apron, the bird and mammal bones in Fig. 204 have been carefully cut, shaped and polished. The various shapes illustrate the desires of their makers. These bone beads did not seem to be used as complete necklaces but were scattered at random with other beads. The longer ones at the bottom, though highly polished, may have been simply bone tubes. Two of the beads at center are most unusual. They have been made to hang vertically. The small bell-shaped bead at right center has been bored from elk or deer antler.

We do know that the first settlers on Nightfire brought bone pendants with them but no shellbeads, but pendants remained popular during all phases of occupation. It is impossible accurately to distinguish between the bones used as sweat-scrapers and those intended for ornaments. Judging from the size alone, the bones in Fig. 205 would be too small for sweat-scrapers. Some of them probably served the very necessary function of a woman's head-scratcher. Many broken fragments of the pendants were carved on the surface in various geometric designs. Plain dotted patterns appear most frequently.

The four bone pendants in Fig. 206 were found together. They are not extensively carved but are nicely finished. The three bone beads were in the same deposit. The most unusual discovery in the cache was the group of 32 crystals shown in the picture. They are made from the rhomboidal-shaped calcite formation. Each crystal has been filed or cut with notches so that it can be held on a cord for a necklace. The author knows of no other such bead combinations.

Steatite

Indians in South America, Central America and the southern part of Mexico mined gold and learned to make it into the shapes

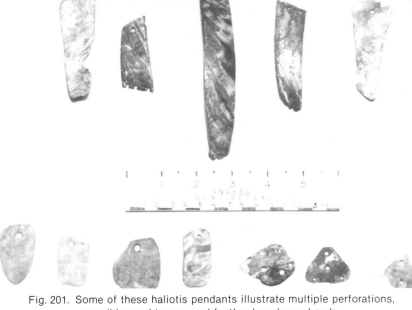

Fig. 201. Some of these haliotis pendants illustrate multiple perforations, possibly used to suspend feather bangles or beads.

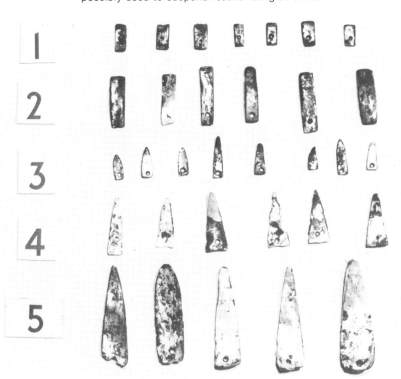

Fig. 202. Smaller cuts of abalone shell.

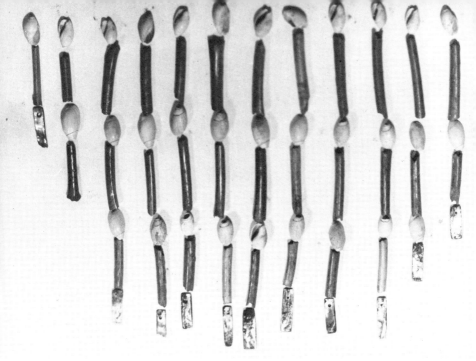

Fig. 203. Birdbone and shell in apron design.

Fig. 204. Birdbone beads were worn in many sizes and styles.

and patterns their artists conceived. The Mayans and Aztecs seemed to value jade more than gold. It seems odd that the people living in the middle of the California gold country, the Shastas at Yreka and the Karoks of the Happy camp region, did nothing with gold. A people—so observant of their environment otherwise—would undoubtedly have seen nuggets and small veins of gold in their everyday activity. Apparently the Modocs had no trade in gold or gold-bearing quartz, even though crystals and agates were collected and preserved. A mineral they did work with was steatite.

Steatite, often called soapstone, is soft enough so that it is easily carved, yet it retains an attractive, shiny surface. These qualities made it a favorite material for pipes, ornaments, beads and dishes, in many parts of California. Since it was soft, it was unsuitable for tools used for percussion or wear.

Tribes living in northwest California were fortunate in having steatite nearby. Gunther Island near Eureka became a sort of dispersal center for steatite objects called "slave killers." Two of these stone clubs have been found in the Lower Klamath Lake basin. The one shown in Fig. 207 was found on the north shore. Its purpose must have been truly ceremonial as it would have been easily broken if used as a club or slave killer. The form of an animal is represented with the tail serving as a handle. Ornamental marks have been filed down each side and a groove cut in the back. The club shows no sign of use. The Modoc who once owned it must have been as proud as Ray Mattson of Merrill, Oregon, its present owner.

Nose Pieces

Another use of steatite is illustrated by the nose pieces in Fig. 208. All five of those in row 4 are of this material. Two are light green, others are darker. Row 3 shows a nose ornament made of two dentalia. A single dentalia worn in the nose by the male Modocs was common at the beginning of the historic period. The nose piece at the right in row 3 is made of bone. Row 2 contains two nose ornaments made of light-green jade, an extremely hard

Fig. 205. Bone ornaments or pendants.

Fig. 206. Rare calcite crystal beads found with bone pendants.

substance and also very rare in a natural state. Even rarer is the piece next to number 1 at the top of the figure. This has been fashioned from a quartz crystal, also a very hard substance. When turned in the sun, it gives off beautiful reflections like a gemstone. The author knows of no other such ground-quartz object, although quartz has been found flaked into arrowpoints. All of the nose ornaments pictured except two were in the third-phase level—more than two thousand years old.

Ornamentation

The tiny sharpened bones at the top of Fig. 209 are too fragile for use as fish gorges and seem too small for nose bones. It seems likely that their purpose was for piercing the septum of the nose or for piercing ears. They might also have been used for making tattoos. Indians are said to have used nettle fiber to keep open the newly pierced nose or ears until they healed and the ornament could be put in place. These small, sharp bones would have served even better for this purpose. The cylindrical, chipped obsidian piece beneath the bone needles is believed to be a broken nosepiece.

The flat bone pieces at the bottom of Fig. 209 are made like tiny spatulas, but they are too small to have served as sweat-scrapers. All have been highly polished, yet show no perforation for use as pendants. The small size and shiny condition suggests their use as paint applicators for making face and body designs.

Paint

Three kinds of paint were found at Nightfire village. There was red, made of burned ocher mixed with grease (ktepki), which was very popular and abundant in the early phases. Another type of red was made from the dust inside the pine bark called wakinsh. Of course, none was preserved. A second kind of paint was the white chalk found in each phase, probably carried from one of the numerous exposed diatomite deposits around the lake. The third type, charcoal, was made and mixed with grease at the site.

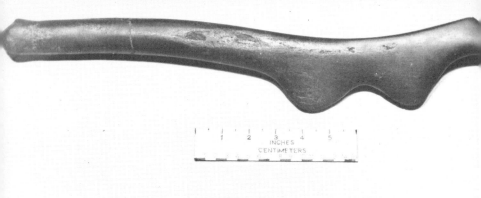

Fig. 207. This steatite "slave killer" was probably traded from the Humboldt Bay region.

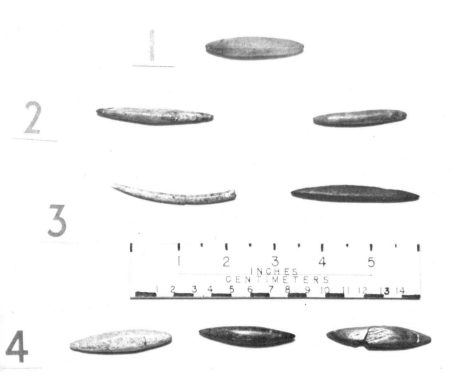

Fig. 208. Nose pieces of crystal, jade, dentalium and steatite.

One informant said that burned plum seeds constituted the best charcoal for paint.

Charcoal was also used in making the permanent tattoos. Some men wore tattoos on the arm as a marker for measuring beads but all girls wore tattoos. Women of the village performed the tattooing art, usually on children. Small slits were made in the skin with a sharp flake of obsidian. Charcoal was then rubbed into the incision and allowed to heal over, leaving the black lines in the skin.

These tattoo marks, as well as being things of beauty, had some ceremonial significance. Girls were carefully watched lest they have the wrong dreams on the night before the tattooing took place. Shasta women, according to Dixon, made a tattoo on the chin resembling the number 111. Early settlers reported Modoc women wearing such marks. Myrtle Caldwell said that her great-grandmother had three marks on her wrist parallel to the arm, in addition to the marks on her chin.

The Place of Eagles

With so many bear teeth in the soil and waste piles, it is hard to believe that the brave hunters of Nightfire could resist decorating themselves with the claws. Unfortunately, the horny material of the claws could not withstand the elements and time, so no such trophies have been found. It is evident, however, that the claws of hawks and eagles were once worn by the people here, Fig. 210. Lower Klamath Lake Basin could still be called "the place of eagles." During summer months, a few can be seen soaring there, and occasionally an eagle on the ground feeding on a squirrel or woodchuck. During winter months, their numbers multiply. Both bald and golden eagles migrate into the basin, evidently to feed at the time of year when snow makes living in the mountains difficult. It is not unusual to be able to count a dozen eagles in the sky north and east of Nightfire.

In the winter of 1977, the National Wildlife Federation conducted a count of eagles in the region adjacent to Nightfire. Surprisingly, 498 of the big birds were counted, making it the largest

Fig. 209. Obsidian nose piece and paint applicators.

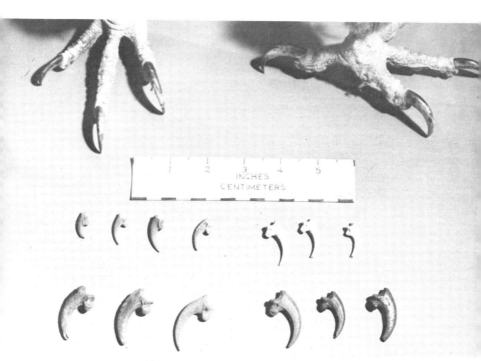

Fig. 210. Eagle and hawk-claw ornaments.

concentration of eagles in the United States outside of Alaska. Rabbits, rodents and fish are preferred food of these predators but the concentration of coots and ducks assure them of a source of winter food. Red-tailed hawks and rough-legged hawks compete with eagles and will attack them in a territorial dispute. The bones in Fig. 210 were found in the three middle phases of the island. The claws have decayed, leaving just the bones to show that they had been used as ornaments. The eagle feet were taken from a dead bird by naturalist, Jim O'Donahue. Bird feathers were probably used for ornamentation at Nightfire, not as a war bonnet but more likely in bangles. The ages have destroyed any evidence of feathers. (The bangle in Fig. 107 is from a cave near Tulelake, California.)

Only Indians are allowed to own eagle feathers. The author may be the only white man in the West to have held a federal permit to hold eagle feathers.

Stone Ornaments

The Klamath Country, which includes the habitat of the Modoc, has very few stones that can be used for making polished stone ornaments. This probably accounts for the scarcity of such objects at Nightfire Village. The three chipped pieces in the top row of Fig. 211 look like arrowpoints but are different in some respects and are regarded as stone pendants. The one at left is of quartz; that in the middle is of agate (burned dark). The piece at right is of obsidian. They were found in a very old phase-one stratum and were used four thousand years before the invention of the bow and arrow. Unlike arrowpoints, the shape is almost cylindrical rather than flat.

The two black, shiny pendants at the top of the figure are of a graphite-like stone. They were found in the fourth-phase level, a much later period than the chipped pieces. The shiny pendant at lower left is made of light green steatite. The two large pieces are of light green serpentine. This material is found in abundance near the town of Happy Camp, California, where the Klamath River cuts through the Siskiyou Mountains. The small, crudely

Fig. 211. Ornaments of stone

Fig. 212. Bent elkhorn ornaments or arm bands.

fashioned bead at the bottom of the figure is made of dark sandstone. The stone pendant at the right is an extremely hard white substance.

Arm Bands

Some culture traits of the Modoc, such as the tobacco pipe or dentalium shell money, could be found in many other tribes of, the West. Others, like the yatish or henwas, were quite localized in adaptation. Another material culture item, which apparently was rather common in the Lower Klamath Lake region—yet unusual, if not unknown in other regions—was the arm band in Fig. 212. Made from thin strips of elkhorn, these ornaments (usually broken) still show skillful detail. The widest fragment found measures 2½ inches. All have perforations drilled at the ends so that they can be joined with cordage. As so-called arm bands have been reported from all sides of the Lower Klamath Lake, they were obviously not the invention of a single individual at Nightfire.

Drills

Bead making and ornament making required the use of drills. Surprisingly, the drills at Nightfire turned out to be different from those in the surrounding areas. There is no logical explanation for this difference. Fig. 213 compares the Nightfire drills with those found in the Cradle Culture at Clear Lake in Fig. 214. It can be observed that they are of obsidian rather than colored stone. Another difference is that few resemble the clock-key shape of the Clear Lake specimen.

Many other drills, and parts of drills not included in the picture, indicate that there was little pride in the tool itself—just something to get the job done. The first row below the vertical figures shows the rounded shape and worn surface of the small borers. They, and perhaps some others in the picture, were mounted on wooden shafts and used with a fire bow. The bottom row shows three natural splinters of obsidian which have been brought in for use as drills or awls.

Fig. 213. Nightfire drills were different and showed signs of use.

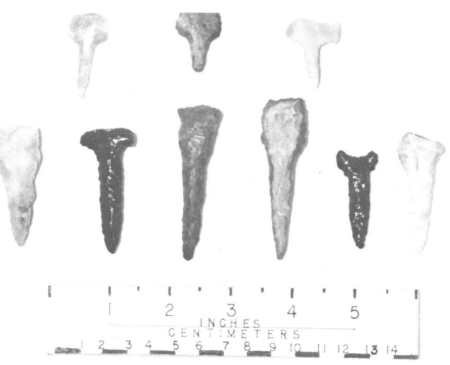

Fig. 214. Drills from the Clear Lake Cradle Culture show little signs of use.

The comparison of the Clear Lake specimen with those of Nightfire raises the question of why they should be so different since they are both Modoc. A difference in age alone does not seem to be a suitable answer. Those in Fig. 213 are obviously drills and show use as drills; the others do not. Could it be that those of the clock-key type, chipped from colored stone, were made for a different purpose, such as for pins, ornaments or projectile points?

Unusual Bone Objects

Some objects used by the Modocs seem to defy description, but names are occasionally given to them because of their shape or the way they may fit into the hand. The double-ended bone objects seen in Fig. 215 appear to be the most exclusive invention of some primitive Thomas Edison at Nightfire. It is certain that no single person is responsible for these objects, nor were they used during any single, given period of time. They have been found in three different phases, representing a span of more than three thousand years. All have been nicely finished. They are pointed at each end but not sharpened like a projectile point or awl. A few have been carved with decorations. There seems to be no source of information relating to these odd-shaped bones. Possibly they were pins to hold the well-known Modoc feather blankets.

The materials shown in Fig. 216 also defy a genuinely accurate description. The carved bone object at the top of the figure has been called a wand because the author saw this term used in a book on archaeology. The two pieces below are made of steatite. The larger one, shaped like a nose piece, in row 3, seems too large and heavy for that purpose. It is over three inches long (8 centimeters) and a little harder than most steatite. The other piece is nicely finished, not a broken fragment. A friend has called it a "fingernail."

The bone objects in row 3 are similar to those at the bottom except that they are made of mammal bone. In the bottom row, all are cut from the breastbones of swans or geese. They show no

Fig. 215. Unique double-ended bone objects.

Fig. 216. Swan breastbone objects with other bones.

decoration or special marking. The third one from right is scalloped as though for use as a comb. Some collectors call these rectangular disks "money"; others term them "pokerchips." None have gone so far as to call them ceremonial pieces. It is possible that any of the objects in Fig. 217 could have been used in a game.

EPILOG

Antiquity of the Modoc

If the ancient Asiatic ancestors were able to return to the Night-fire Island habitat and join their Modoc descendants, they would not have felt greatly handicapped in making a living. True, the invention of the bow and arrow had revolutionized hunting, yet the techniques for making projectiles had changed but little. The elephant, then the bison and wolf, had disappeared, but other animals replaced them. Skins, reeds and grasses were still used for clothing. The methods of cooking were only slightly improved. The development of their extensive vocabulary is an indication of long years of occupation and communication. The survival skills must have been successfully passed along with little change.

The conservatism toward change by the Modoc illustrates that people adapted to their surroundings, rather than trying to change them—and a remarkable adaptation it was. Surviving in periods of drought and cold, they perpetuated a culture pattern that has provided an almost continuous scenario from the period of occupation of North America to the era of European contact. It is remarkable that the setting for the entire story took place in the same region. These fierce people, called "primitive pragmatists" by one anthropologist, were able to defend and hold their territory against the pressure of the aggressive Paiutes, the Shastas and their Pit River neighbors. Meacham suggested that a major conflict with the Klamaths took place but there is little evidence of this beyond the normal raids and forays between villages.

As scientific research continues, new information concerning early man will be revealed, new sites found, and possibly greater age will be proved for the time period that human beings have lived in North America. Whatever else may be discovered, it seems doubtful that any place will be found that was continuously occupied longer than the Modoc homeland. The sands of Nightfire have shown the connection between the Cradle Culture and the Clear Lake-Lost River Circle with the Modoc. Each phase blends with the next, with interruptions only when lake levels forced evacuation from the island. The last phase showed a brief but marked change—the entry of the European.

The Decline

Early contact with the white man can usually be measured by the appearance of tradegoods such as glass, copper or iron. The numbers of Modocs appear to have declined markedly about 800 B.P., before the tradegoods arrived. Even then the amount of such goods left on Modoc sites was meager compared with that owned by the neighboring Klamaths. Most of the heavily occupied shores of Lower Klamath Lake had been deserted. Only a few village sites were described to Gatschet by his Indian informants in 1885.

Climate could hardly have affected the resourceful Modoc. More likely, a combination of enemy attrition and disease caused the population reduction. One small part of Nightfire even showed a family had returned to the creekside for a brief period after 800 years of abandonment. The people of the south, called "Moadoci" by the Klamaths, had not lost the old spirit, however, as events leading to the war with the United States Army later proved.

APPENDIX

Birds of the Klamath Basin National Wildlife Refuges
U.S. Fish and Wildlife

The following list contains species recorded on or near the refuges. Symbols indicating the relative abundance of each species are tabulated as follows: a—abundant, c—common, u—uncommon, o—occasional, r—rare.

If a species is apt to be limited to a particular habitat type, location keys (1 to 5) are provided to indicate where the species may be seen: 1—Upper Klamath, 2—Clear Lake, 3—Lower Klamath, 4—Tule Lake, 5—Klamath Forest.

	March-April	June-August	Sept.-Nov.	Dec.-Feb.	Nesting Locally
Whistling Swan	c		c	a	
Trumpeter Swan	r			r	
Canada Goose	a	c	a	c	yes
Black Brant			o		
Emperor Goose	r		o		
White-fronted Goose	a	o	a	u	
Snow Goose	a	o	a	u	
Blue Goose	r		r		
Ross' Goose	u	o	u	o	
Mallard	a	a	a	c	yes
Gadwall	c	c	c	o	yes
Pintail	a	c	a	c	yes
Green-winged Teal	c	o	a	o	yes
Blue-winged Teal	o	u	r		yes
Cinnamon Teal	c	a	c	r	yes
American Widgeon	a	o	a	u	yes
Shoveler	a	c	a	c	yes
Wood Duck	u	u	u		yes
Redhead	c	a	c	u	yes

239

	March-April	June-August	Sept.-Nov.	Dec.-Feb.	Nesting Locally
Ring-necked Duck	u	u	u	u	yes
Canvasback	c	u	c	u	yes
Greater Scaup	o		o		
Lesser Scaup	c	u	a	c	yes
Common Goldeneye	c	r	u	c	
Barrow's Goldeneye	o			o	
Bufflehead	c	o	c	u	
Oldsquaw			o		
White-winged Scoter	r		o	r	
Surf Scoter			r	r	
Ruddy Duck	a	c	a	u	yes
Hooded Merganser	u	u	u	u	yes
Common Merganser	c	o	a	c	yes
Red-breasted Merganser	r				
Common Loon	u	o	u	r	
Red-necked Grebe- 1,5		u			yes
Horned Grebe	o	o			
Eared Grebe	c	a	a	u	yes
Western Grebe	c	a	a	u	yes
Pied-billed Grebe	c	c	c	u	yes
White Pelican	c	c	c		yes
Double-crested Cormorant	c	c	c	r	yes
Great Blue Heron	c	c	c	c	yes
Green Heron- 1	o	o			
Common Egret	c	c	c	r	yes
Snowy Egret	u	c	u		yes
Black-crowned Night Heron	c	c	c	u	yes
Least Bittern	r	r	r		yes
American Bittern	c	r	u	o	yes
White-faced Ibis	u	u	r		yes
Sandhill Crane	u	u	u		yes
Virginia Rail	o	o	o	r	yes
Sora	o	o	o	r	yes
American Coot	a	a	a	c	yes

	March-April	June-August	Sept.-Nov.	Dec.-Feb.	Nesting Locally
Snowy Plover	r	r			yes
Killdeer	c	c	c	c	yes
Black-bellied Plover	o	o	o	o	
Ruddy Turnstone	o		o		
Common Snipe	u	u	u	r	yes
Long-billed Curlew	u	u	o		yes
Whimbrel	r		r		
Spotted Sandpiper	o	u	o		yes
Solitary Sandpiper	u	o	u		
Willet	u	c	u		yes
Greater Yellowlegs	c	u	c	o	
Lesser Yellowlegs	o	o	o		
Knot			r		
Pectoral Sandpiper	r		r		
Least Sandpiper	a	u	a		
Dunlin	c	o	o		
Long-billed Dowitcher	c	c	a	o	
Stilt Sandpiper		r	r		
Western Sandpiper	c	c	c		
Marbled Godwit	o	r	r		
Sanderling	r	r			
American Avocet	c	a	c	r	yes
Black-necked Stilt	u	c	o		yes
Red Phalarope	o		o		
Wilson's Phalarope	o	c	o		yes
Northern Phalarope	u	o	u		
Herring Gull			o	o	
California Gull	c	a	o	u	yes
Ring-billed Gull	c	a	c	c	yes
Bonaparte's Gull	o	u	u		
Forster's Tern	c	a	c		yes
Caspian Tern	u	c	u		yes
Black Tern	u	a	u		yes
Mourning Dove	c	c	c	o	yes

	March-April	June-August	Sept.-Nov.	Dec.-Feb.	Nesting Locally
Barn Owl	u	u	u	u	yes
Screech Owl- 1,5	o	o	o	o	yes
Great Horned Owl	u	u	u	u	yes
Pygmy Owl- 1,5	o	o	o	o	yes
Burrowing Owl		o	o		yes
Great Gray Owl- 1,5	r	r	r	r	yes
Long-eared Owl- 1,5	r	r	r	r	
Short-eared Owl- 1,5	u	c	c	c	yes
Saw-whet Owl- 1,5	r	r	r	r	yes
Steller's Jay- 1,5	u	c	c	u	yes
Scrub Jay- 2	u	u	u	u	yes
Black-billed Magpie	c	c	c	c	yes
Common Raven	o	r	o	o	
Goshawk- 1,5	o	o	o	r	yes
Sharp-shinned Hawk	o	o	o	r	yes
Cooper's Hawk	o	o	o	o	
Red-tailed Hawk	c	u	c	c	yes
Swainson's Hawk	o	o	o		
Rough-legged Hawk	c		c	c	
Ferruginous Hawk			o		
Golden Eagle	u	o	u	c	yes
Bald Eagle	c	o	u	a	yes
Marsh Hawk	c	c	c	c	yes
Osprey- 1,5	o	o	r		yes
Prairie Falcon	u	o	o	o	yes
Peregrine Falcon	o	r	o	r	yes
Pigeon Hawk	u	o	u	o	yes
Sparrow Hawk	c	u	c	c	yes

SOURCES

Anderson, Lynn, "Klamath Basketry." Unpublished report, University of Oregon, 1976.

Bedwell, Steven F., *Fort Rock Basin Prehistory and Environment*. University of Oregon Books, Eugene, Oregon, 1973.

Bennett, Kenneth A., "Sacral Rachischisis on Modoc Skeletons." *American Journal of Physical Anthropology*, May 1972.

Bordaz, Jacques, "First Tools of Mankind." *Natural History Magazine*, Jan., Feb., 1959.

Copeland, Margaret Ayr, "An Analysis of Modoc Basketry." M.A. Thesis, University of Washington. Published by S.S. Johnson Foundation, Redmond, Oregon, 1970.

Coville, Frederick V., "Wocus, Primitive Food of the Klamath Indians." National Museum Report, 1902.

Cressman, Luther S., *An Approach to the Study of Far Western Prehistory: Early Man*. Museum of Natural History Publication, No. 20, University of Oregon, Eugene, Oregon, 1973.

————, and collaborators, *Archaeological Researches in the Northern Great Basin*. Carnegie Institutions of Washington Publication. No. 538, 1942.

————, Haag, W.G., and Laughlin, W.S., *Klamath Prehistory*. American Philosophical Society, Vol. 46, Part 4, 1956.

————, and collaborators, *Culture Sequences at The Dalles, Oregon*. American Philosophical Society, Vol. 50, Part 10, 1960.

————, "Odell Lake Site, A new Paleo-Indian Camp Site in Oregon." *American Antiquity*, Vol. 14, No. 1, July 1948.

————, *Prehistory of the Far West, Homes of Vanished Peoples*. University of Utah Press, Salt Lake City, Utah, 1977.

Curtin, Jeremiah, *Myths of the Modocs: Indian Legends of the Northwest*. Benjamin Blom, Inc., Publishers, New York, 1971.

————, Unpublished manuscript. Bureau American Ethnography, M.S. No. 1299, Washington, D.C.

Deuel, Leo, *Conquistadors Without Swords*. St. Martin's Press, Inc., New York, 1967.

Dixon, Roland B., *The Shasta*. The Huntington, California Expedition Report, American Museum of Natural History, 1907.

Farb, Peter, *Man's Rise to Civilization*. E.P. Dutton and Co., New York, 1968.

Gatschet, Albert S., *The Klamath Indians of Southwestern Oregon*. Contribution to North American Ethnology, Vol. 2, 1890.

Heizer, R.F., and Whipple, M.A., *The California Indians*. University of California Press, Berkeley, California, 1973.

Howe, Carrol B., *Ancient Tribes of the Klamath Country*. Binfords and Mort, Portland, Oregon, 1968.

Jewett, Stanley G., "Klamath Basin Wildlife Refuges." *Wildlife Leaflet No. 238*, U.S. Department of Interior, Chicago, Illinois, 1943.

Johnson, LeRoy, "The Klamath Basin Archaeological Project," Descriptive Proposal to the National Science Foundation from Oregon Museum of Natural History, Eugene, Oregon, June 1, 1970.

————, "Obsidian Hydration Rate For California and Oregon." *Science*, American Association For the Advancement of Science, Vol. 165, Sept. 26, 1969.

Joyce, T. Athol, *South American Archaeology*. G.P. Putnam's Sons, New York, 1912.

Kelly, Isabel T., *Ethnography of the Surprise Valley Paiute*. University of California Publications in Archaeology and Ethnography, Berkeley, California, 1932.

Kirk, Ruth, *The Oldest Man in North America*. Harcourt Brace Jovanovich, Inc., New York, 1974.

Kroeber, A.L., *Handbook of the Indians of California*. California Book Co. Ltd., Berkeley, California, reprinted 1967.
Lemke, R.W., and others, "Geologic Setting of the Glacier Peak and Mazama Ashbed Markers in West Central Montana." *Geological Survey Bulletin* 1395-H, U.S. Government Printing Office, Washington, D.C., 1975.
Locke, Justin, "Lost Kingdom in Indian Mexico." *National Geographic Magazine*, Oct. 1952.
Mason, Otis T., *Aboriginal American Basketry*. U.S. National Museum Report, 1902.
Meacham, A.B., *Wigwam and Warpath*. John P. Dale and Co., Boston, 1875.
Michels, Joseph, "Progress Report on Obsidian Hydration Dating." 65th annual meeting of American Anthropological Association, Pittsburgh, Pennsylvania, 1967.
Murray, Keith A., *The Modocs and Their War*. The University of Oklahoma Press, Norman, Oklahoma, 1965.
Ogden, Peter Skene, *Snake Country Journal*, 1826-27, The Hudson's Bay Record Society, London, 1961.
Randle, Keith; and Goles, and Kittleman, "Geochemical and Petrological Characterization of Ash Samples From Cascade Range Volcanoes." *Quaternary Research*, Vol. 1, No. 2, April 1971.
Ray, Verne F., *Primitive Pragmatists*. University of Washington Press, Seattle, 1963.
Rice, David, *The Windust Phase in Lower Snake River Region Prehistory*. Report of Investigations No. 50, Washington State University, Pullman, Washington, 1972.
Schulz, Paul E., *Indians of Lassen Volcanic National Park and Vicinity*. Loomis Museum Association, Mineral, California, 1954.
Spier, Leslie, *Klamath Ethnography*. University of California Publications in American Archaeology and Ethnography, No. 30, 1930.
Strong, Emory, *Stone Age in the Great Basin*. Binfords and Mort, Portland, Oregon, 1969.
Vogel, Larry, "Preliminary Report on Nightfire Island Pollen Samples." Unpublished, 1976.
Wheat, Joe Ben, "Lifeways of Early Man in North America." *Arctic Anthropology*, Vol. 8, No. 2, University of Wisconsin Press, 1971.
Wormington, H.M., *Ancient Man in North America*. Denver Museum of Natural History, 1957.
————, "Comments on Early Man in North America," 1960-70. *Arctic Anthropology*, Vol. 8, No. 2, University of Wisconsin Press, 1971.

Information by Interview:

Mrs. O.T. Anderson (Klamath Indian)—native foods
James A. Blaisdell (National Park Service)—bighorn sheep
Bruce Bradley (archaeologist)—flint knapping
Myrtle Caldwell (Indian descendant)—marriage customs
David Cole (archaeologist)—marriage customs
Alfred Collier (historian)—fishing methods
Del Davis (mineralogist)—Northwest bolas
Mathew DelFatti (collector)—basketry
James O. DeVore (collector)—Lost River Circle
Jim Dixon (cowboy)—Indian foods
Dr. David Easterla (zoologist)—birds and animals
Patti Easterla (Modoc descendant)—Modoc history
Wren Frain (Shasta Indian)—Indian houses
Leroy Gienger (pioneer)—plant foods

Paul Haertel (superintendent Lava Beds National Monument)—bighorn
  sheep
MacDonald Heebner (naturalist)—pictographs
Dr. LeRoy Johnson (archaeologist)—Peruvian bolas
Joseph Kennedy (park superintendent)—super-nova pictograph
Glen Kircher (fisherman)—fish runs
Dr. Laurence Kittleman (geologist)—obsidian identification
Charles Mitchell (Favell Museum)—atlatl weights
Charles Ogle (pioneer)—Indian foods
Mrs. Amy Lenz Royce (Klamath Indian)—Indian foods
Robert Rock (rock collector)—mineral sources
William Skeen (Modoc Indian)—canoes, foods
Ann Swithinbank (research assistant)—Mazama ash

INDEX

247

Mortars, bedrock, 50, 51, 53; lazy
  wife, 33; manufacture, 52, 54, 56;
  old people's, 66, 67
Mourning customs, 187, 188
Mule deer, 91
Mushrooms, 117, 122
Mussel shells, 209, 210
Mythology, 171-177

N

National Geographic Magazine, 49
National Science Foundation, 15
Nettles, 118, 121, 122
Net weights, 150, 151, 152
Nevada Historical Society, 60, 61, 72,
  73
Norsemen, 19
Nose pieces, 228, 233

O

Obsidian, 71; dance, 202, 203;
  hydration, 41, 77, 78, 79; sources,
  75, 76; splinters, 194, 195; trade,
  212
Odell, Ida, 206
O'Donahue, Jim, 37
Ogden, Peter Skene, 9, 160, 188
Ogle, Charlie, 39
Ogle, Selden, 39
Old people's food, 68
Olivella, 211
Orcutt, Theodore, 72
Oregon Museum of Natural History,
  15
Oregon State University, 165
Ornamentation, 223-225
Otter, 92

P

Pacific flyway, 37
Paint, 225; deposits, 191, 192
Paiute Indians, 36
Peccary, 21
Pestles, 120
Petroglyphs, 179-181
Phragmites, 121
Pictographs, 179-181
Piel, Alice Applegate, 184
Pipes, 124, 139; bone, 128, 129; filter,
  130
Pit River Indians, 199
Pollen, 97
Pollock, Norma, 145
Power quest, 177-181

Projectile points, 89, 96; Cascade, 69;
  corner notch, 86; manufacture, 69,
  70, 71
Puffballs, 120
Purse, elkhorn, 215

Q

Quern, 30; mortars, 30, 32

R

Rabbit, 95
Ray, Verne, 199
Religion, 171-190
Roasting ovens, 64
Robe, deerskin, 93
Rock art, 179
Rogue River Indians, 23
Royce, Mrs. Len, 109

S

Sacramento River, 6
Salmon, 141-146
Salt Cave, 134
Sampson, Dr. Garth, 16, 17, 98
Sandia-type point, 31
San Dieguito culture, 33
Sandstone, 132, 133
Schultz, Paul, 199
Sequim, Washington, 22
Serpentine, 229, 230
Shafer, Juanna and Terry, 95
Shaman, 192-197
Shasta Indians, 23, 55, 148, 201
Shasta Mountain, 1, 172, 211
Sheep, bighorn, 84-86
Sheepy Creek, 5, 142
Shotwell, Dr. Arnold, 12, 15
Sioux Indians, 36
Skeen, Bill, 107, 153
Skull trophies, 182, 188, 199
Slave killer, 226
Sloth, ground, 21, 25, 29
Smithsonian Institution, 50, 51
Smoking, 125, 126
Southern Methodist University, 129,
  131
Spier, Leslie, 138, 166
Splinter awls, 121, 123
Spoon, 213
Sprague River, 150
Steatite, 140, 141, 223, 226
Stone weights, 65
Stuart, H.H., 25
Suckers, 156-159, 162
Summer house, 106
Super Nova, 180